VISIT OUR ONLINE SHOP

shop.keypublishing.com/petewater

KEY

hop

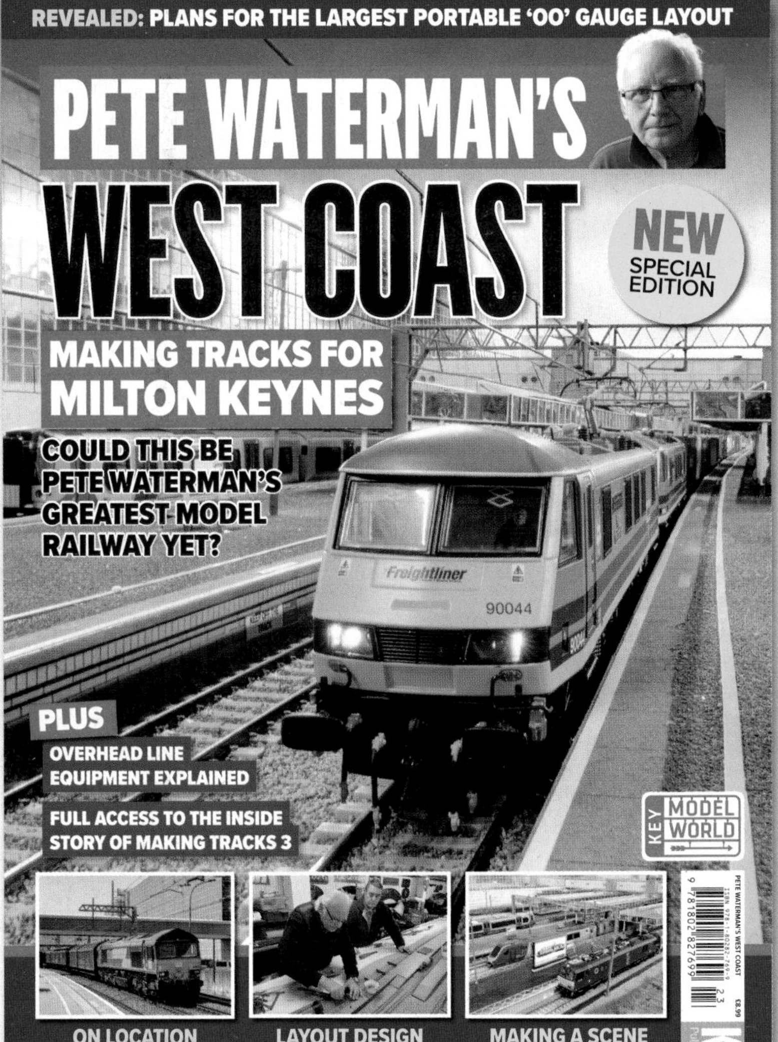

In ... to his Gr... n 2022, Pet... oup are taking on their biggest challenge yet. The team are building a scale model of Milton Keynes Central Station for the third Making Tracks event in Chester Cathedral this summer. This brand-new model railway is a 64ft long reconstruction of the West Coast Main Line city station with bespoke buildings, structure catenary and much more. This bookazine provides an in-depth look at the creation of this stunning layout covering the history of the station, construction of the layout and exclusive behind the scenes stories which make this a model railway to inspire every railway enthusiast.

IF YOU ARE INTERESTED IN **MODEL RAIL** YOU MAY ALSO WANT TO ORDER...

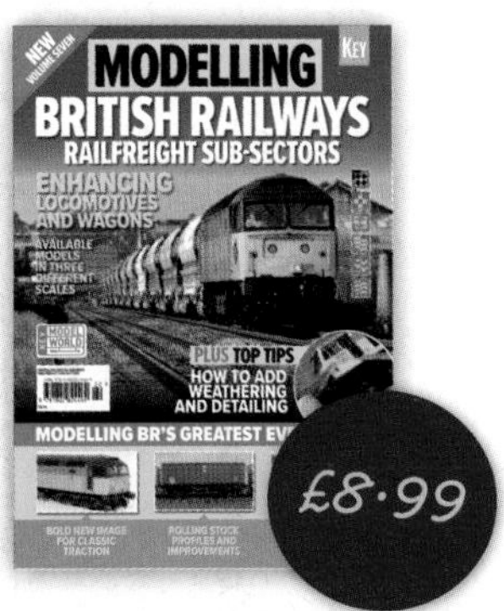

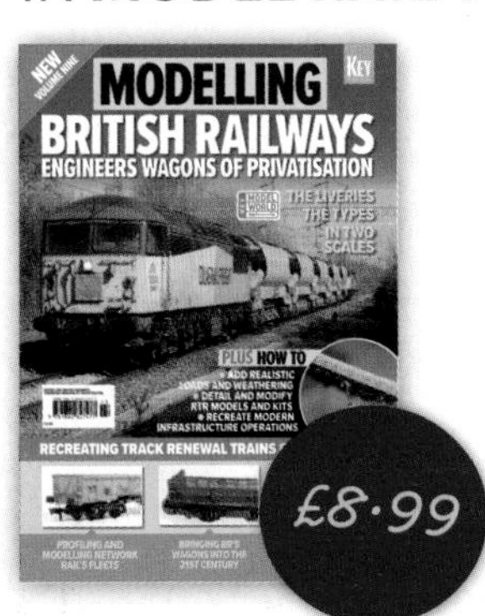

FREE P&P* when you order online at...

shop.keypublishing.com/petewatermanwestcoast

Call +44 (0)1780 480404 *(Monday to Friday 9am-5.30pm GMT)*

Also available from **W.H Smith** and all leading newsagents.

**Free 2nd class P&P on all UK & BFPO orders. Overseas charges apply.*

What's inside...

Lakeside is an action packed 'OO' modern image layout created by Graham Foulston.

Clever modelling by Mark Wilson has resulted in a delightful slice of Swindon's famous works in 'OO'.

North Cornwall Brewery – an imaginary Southern Region setting in 'OO'.

EDITORIAL
Editor: Mike Wild
Publication Editor: Nick Brodrick
Assistant Editor: Mark Chivers
Sub Editor: Andy Roden
Senior Designer: Steve Diggle
Design: SJmagic DESIGN SERVICES, India

REGISTERED OFFICE
Units 1-4, Gwash Way Industrial Estate, Ryhall Road, Stamford, Lincs PE9 1XP

PRINTING
Precision Colour Printing Ltd, Haldene, Halesfield, Telford, Shropshire TF7 4QQ.

ADVERTISING
Advertising: Brodie Baxter
Email: brodie.baxter@keypublishing.com
Tel: 01780 755131 **Fax:** 01780 757261
Advertising Production: Rebecca Duffy
Tel: 01780 755131
Fax: 01780 757261
Email: rebecca.duffy@keypublishing.co.uk

PUBLISHING
Publisher: Mark Elliott
Tel: 01780 755131
Fax: 01780 757261
Email: mark.elliott@keypublishing.com

Group CEO: Adrian Cox
Head of Advertising: Brodie Baxter
Head of Production: Janet Watkins
Head of Content Management: Finbarr O'Reilly
Chief Digital Officer: Vicky Macey
Chief Customer Officer: Gaynor Hemingway-Gibbs
Chief Content & Commercial Officer: Mark Elliott

KEY PUBLISHING
Key Publishing Ltd,
Units 1-4, Gwash Way Industrial Estate
Ryhall Road Stamford, Lincs PE9 1XP

The Gresley Beat

Busy LNER main line action makes this epic layout a perpetual exhibition favourite. **CLIFF PARSONS** explains why and how this faithful slice of the East Coast Main Line was created.

PHOTOGRAPHY, TREVOR JONES

Right: **With its distinctive 'Cod's Mouth' and smokebox door open, 'A4' 2512 *Silver Fox* receives fitter's attention on in the company of a 'C12' 4-4-2T, 'J50' 0-6-0T and 'N2' 0-6-2T. The 'Top Shed' structures have been made using original scale drawings.**

Below: **Gresley 'A4' 4495 *Golden Fleece* powers north on the low-level fast lines as an Ivatt 'C1' 4-4-2 ambles along above with a rake of horse boxes. The bridge features a static representation of the North London line with an LMS 'Jinty' 0-6-0T apparently heading eastwards. The scene is dominated by a stunning re-creation of the former Necropolis Railway's Cemetery Station.**

IT'S THE kind of tail-chasing layout many of us dream about. Multiple running levels, a full-size locomotive depot and goods marshalling yard, served by 24 roads of fiddle yard jammed with up to 46 trains… There's art-deco inter-city expresses, a 90-wagon empty coal train and articulated suburban 'stoppers', plus much, much more.

Simply put, The Gresley Beat is awe inspiring.

Inspired by the legendary Apple Green and Garter Blue locomotives of Sir Nigel Gresley in their London North Eastern Railway pomp, the 465sq/ft ensemble depicts the East Coast Main Line immediately north of King's Cross.

The track plan depicts four main lines: Up and Down passenger, Up and Down goods, and one end-to-end serving the shed, turntable and the carriage sidings.

The bustling nature of The Gresley Beat has echoes of the Model Railway Club's similarly impressive 2mm scale contemporary, Copenhagen Fields. But with the 4mm scale layout only

Viewed down Taylor's End, adjacent to the Percy Arms, an ex-Great Central Railway 'Director' passes on the main line while a 'J50' 0-6-0T leads a goods on the upper level.

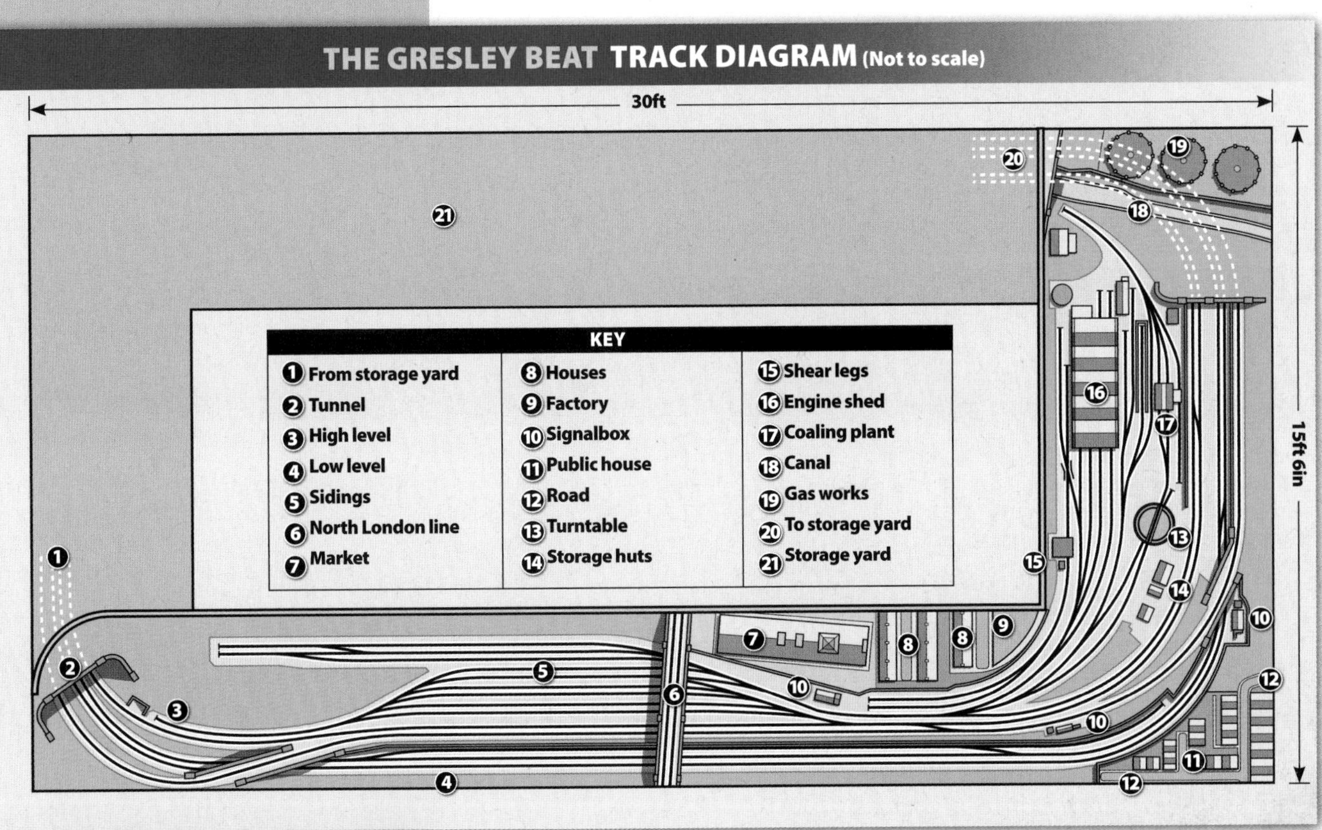

Below: **An 'Up' express coasts downhill towards King's Cross behind GNR pioneer 'Pacific' 1470N *Great Northern*, while 'A4' *Golden Fleece* gets into its stride with the Edinburgh Waverley-bound 'Coronation', complete with the unique ex-North Eastern Railway dynamometer car at its head.**

measuring 8ft longer than its miniature 'cousin', it has required a degree of shrewd compression and compromise in order to incorporate the key classic features between Gasworks Tunnel and Oakley Park Tunnels, namely 'Top Shed', the Skew Bridge Flyover and the North London Line.

The sense of place created with these well-known locations is therefore crucial to the success of the 'Beat', especially as there is no station that would readily pinpoint the region, even if not specific area.

"Prominent features include the North London architecture with stone features around yellow brick structures," says the layout's visionary Cliff Parsons. "As The Gresley Beat is an urban setting there are a large number of buildings and structures and many hours were invested in building of this for the layout."

Although the model has been deliberately created to entertain exhibition visitors, "bearing in mind that most of the paying public just want to see trains running… detail has been added wherever possible including railings around the openings to basements, barrels being unloaded outside the Percy Arms, period adverts, street signs and lamps".

A scene of Victorian properties has been beautifully captured by master architectural modeller Geoff Taylor and is far more popular with viewers than its 'corner filler' status might otherwise suggest.

> *"Most of the paying public just want to see trains running."*
> **CLIFF PARSONS**

"The streets are all finished with stone setts", Cliff continues, "while the eagle-eyed will be able to spot features such as a telephone box modelled with the door open, washing hanging in the garden of the town houses, street names and a period figures in typical street poses." »

Former Great Central Railway Robinson 'J11' 0-6-0 5986 plods by Gas Works signalbox in this wonderfully detailed scene, including point rodding and signal wires.

The majority of buildings are MDF shells covered with Plasticard, detailed and painted. Most of the retaining walls made from artist's foam-board which allows the arch shapes to be cut and removed easily, before being covered with plastic card, drain and gas pipes and other details.

Eclectic mix

As important as creating the inter-war urban environment of King's Cross has been, it would be nothing without the plethora of trains that parade around it.

After all, it was "started some 30 years ago with the idea of showing the work of Gresley's locomotives and stock in a realistic setting and running full length trains at scale speeds".

That wasn't necessarily an easy prospect when Cliff embarked on his adventure.

Ready-to-run 'OO' gauge LNER locomotives and rolling stock were "fairly thin on the ground", he recalls, which called for a many hours of kit and scratch building from a variety of helpers.

The welcome arrival of Hornby's detailed 4-6-2s in the early years of 2000s opened the door for a steady stream of near-layout-ready stock, which shows no sign of slowing given

Heljan 'O2' 2-8-0 3965 hefts a rake of bogie brick wagons past the 'Top Shed' while a scratch-built 'P2' gleams as it takes coal.

the fresh development 'Quad Art' carriages (to name but one recent example); something scarcely believable 30 year ago.

Gresley locomotives, as befits the layout's name, predominate: 'N2' 0-6-2Ts, 'J50' 0-6-0T, 'K3' and 'V4' 2-6-0s, 'A1', 'A3' and 'A4' 4-6-2s, as well as the more exotic 'W1' 4-6-4, 'P1' and 'P2' 2-8-2s, plus the mammoth 'U1' 2-8-0+0-8-2395. Modeller's licence has been freely used to bring the unique Garratt down from its banking duties over the Woodhead Route in South Yorkshire!

There's also a place for more elderly locomotives inherited from the Great Northern Railway, such as Ivatt's graceful 'C2' 4-4-2s and 'C12' 4-4-2Ts, which can be found on 'semi-fasts' and horsebox specials. There are also cameo appearances by Great Central Railway 'J11' 0-6-0s, 'D11' 4-4-0s and Great Eastern Railway 'N7' 0-6-2Ts.

Highlights of the 'A1', 'A3' and 'A4' hauled expresses include the streamlined 'Silver Jubilee' and 'West Riding' plus a 'Coronation' set with the LNER's dynamometer car at the front of the formation, all using Golden Age Models products.

When locomotives aren't hauling trains, some can be seen in between duties on 'Top Shed', where Cliff once frequented as a childhood trainspotter.

Above: **A busy moment near Oakleigh Park Tunnel (also known as Barnet Tunnel) as an 'Atlantic'-hauled string of horseboxes weaves away from London. Below, 'A3' 2746 *Fairway* is in charge of a travelling post office train, while the distance, a 'P1' approaches with private owner coal wagons.**

Left: **The Gresley Beat was designed to keep viewers entertained by mixing non-stop train action with a detailed urban landscape. The 'Silver Jubilee' is glimpsed leaving King's Cross.**

Summer bliss

Other memories also played a part in determining the time of year that the layout is set. Cliff chose late summer, "so I can run both holiday trains and football specials".

That determined the dry, brown grass effect created using teddy bear fur, with Woodlands Scenics foliage applied to represent weeds and shrubs at the lineside. The area between the raw edge of the fur fabric and the trackbed is then covered with PVA and static grass applied to mask any unsightly joins.

The base for the scenery was constructed using 3mm ply formers, covered with 1in wide interwoven strips of cardboard, overlaid in turn with plaster bandage (using a 50:50 water and PVA solution to set it to the required profile).

Trees near the front of the layout are a mixture of hand-made twisted wire examples covered with hot melt glue. The branches are painted in a subtle variation of colours depending on the species, and 'leafed' with Woodland Scenics foliage.

A mixture of sea foam 'forest in a box' type specimens fill areas near the backscene (the latter painted by none other than *The Who* lead singer Roger Daltry).

Plain track on scenic areas is SMP code 75 bullhead, with pointwork made from copper-clad sleepers, while Peco code 75 flat-bottom rail provided a cost-effective and durable way of laying the fiddle yard. "After all, there is no need for scale track in off-scene areas," Cliff remarks. »

Another action-packed scene as GNR 'Q2' 0-8-0 3455 crosses paths with 'Mikado' 2394 on the high-level lines, as a GER 'N7' 0-6-2T passes below with a suburban train for King's Cross. Note the cabbages growing in the adjacent allotment.

Gresley beasts at Gas Works Tunnel. Heading south with loaded coal wagons is 'P1' 2-8-2 2394 while exiting on the right is one-off Garratt 2395 with a mixed goods headed by cattle wagons. St Pancras station and the now-dismantled gasometers dominate the skyline.

"Although the layout is 4mm:1ft scale, I used 2mm:1ft scale ballast for the scenic area," he adds. "This was applied in the normal way but with the webbing on the flexible track removed and the sleepers repositioned to the correct distance. This also allows daylight between the rail and the ballast to be achieved once the latter is tamped down."

The signalboxes and yard lamps on the layout were all built by Mick Nicholson using a variety of materials. The signals are constructed from brass using etched signal arms or scratch built.

Team effort

As well as those already mentioned, Cliff is keen to thank his friends Len Smith, Brian and Barbara Longhurst, Steve Banks, Rupert Brown and Malcolm Barnsley, as well as "long-suffering wife" Barbara, for their assistance in creating this incredible layout.

After many years delighting more than 100,000 people on the exhibition circuit, including mainland Europe, 'The Beat' is now destined to play a starring role at the future *Ashford International Model Railway Education Centre* (*AIMREC*) having been recently bequeathed to the project.

The aim of AIMREC is to preserve important layouts for the nation and use them to educate school parties and under-graduates about Britain's heritage and the part railways played in the industrial revolution.

Happily, therefore, the future of this epic LNER showpiece is secure. ■

READ MORE

Visit www.keymodelworld.comfeatures

The Gresley Beat at its breath-taking best. A host of modelling disciplines blended together to create a harmonious cityscape.

Coniston Lake

Prototype reality meets modelling fiction in the miniature 1960s Cumbrian world created by **MIKE POWELL** inspired by visits to the former Coniston branch.

PHOTOGRAPHY, MIKE WILD

It might not look prototypical, but divided portions of the 'Lakes Express' could be seen behind 'Duchesses'. Stanier '8P, No. 46238 *City of Carlisle* rolls into Coniston Lake before handing its modest train over for a run to Coniston Town behind a tank engine.

"IMAGINATION IS A WONDERFUL THING", says Mike Powell. His loft layout, Coniston Lake shows such creativity in spades.

While he concedes that the London Midland Region themed model is "fictional" there are plenty of prototypical elements that give it life, meaning and therefore believability.

A visit to the original Coniston station site didn't offer Mike much in the way of helpful research material; the stylish overall roof station having been demolished in 1968, five years after the last trains ran. Only the footbridge survives, albeit in a private garden in Berkshire! Even though, suitably inspired by the local history of the area he grew up in, Mike sought to base a layout around the former South Lakeland jewel.

"Rather than model the prototype terminus, I decided to base my layout on Coniston station building, but in a different location."

This approach enabled him to create a fantasy railway system.

"My objective has always been to reflect the railways of West Cumbria in the 1960s," he explains. "Rather than model the prototype terminus, I decided to base my layout on Coniston station building, but in a different location.

Beneath the atmospheric overall roof, '8F' 48151 clanks through Coniston Lake as 'Black Five' 44709 approaches with a mixed freight from the south.

> *"My objective has always been to reflect the railways of West Cumbria in the 1960s."*
>
> **MIKE POWELL**

"Instead of being at the far end of a single-track branch line. I have a double track secondary main line calling at a major rural station, which is also the junction for a branch line to Coniston Town. I have to acknowledge that my imaginary main line would have faced steep gradients and prodigious amounts of tunnelling on its journey north – but that's not my problem!"

The station was relocated from high above the town to the southern end of Coniston Water, similar to Lakeside on Windermere, hence the name: Coniston Lake.

The journey

The extensive layout has its origins in something much smaller – a 4ft x 2ft terminus diorama created in the early 2000s with a compressed version of the Furness Railway's original Consiton station building, complete with its ornate portico and integral goods shed, scratch built from embossed plastic sheeting.

An attic conversion opened-up an opportunity to break free from the 'four by two' and Coniston Lake became the terminus station of new out and back layout begun in 2015, later developing into a through station

Through trains from the north pass beneath a typical FR grey stone overbridge overlooked by a substantial retaining wall above which is the small town of Coniston Lake.

Although other key railway structures scratch built, several of the town buildings are embossed plastic sheeting laminated onto Metcalfe card kits "to speed up the process".

Coniston Lake station has three platforms: Up and Down main with a platform loop for branch line trains to Coniston Town.

Set against a broad panorama of Coniston Water, trains then pass Coniston Lake signalbox, after which is the start of the branch to Coniston Town. This rises on a steep gradient to cross the main line further on.

The Motive Power Depot on the other side of the track is based on the depot at Moor Row in West Cumbria and is overlooked by Railway Terrace.

Between the depot and the main line, a goods loop holds slow freight trains heading north, looped so they don't impede faster passenger trains on the steep gradients »

The starter signal is 'off' for Carlisle Kingmoor-allocated 'Clan' 72008 *Clan MacLeod* at Coniston Lake. The scratch-built station with modified Hornby kit-built footbridge dominate the skyline against the backdrop of Coniston Water.

ahead. Some freight trains stop in the station to receive a banker, usually a Fairburn '4MT' 2-6-4T as at Shap.

Beyond is pastoral countryside as the main line disappears from view beneath the Coniston Town branch, held aloft by a steel bridge based on one at Rowrah in West Cumbria.

Pick 'n' mix

This skewed reality of Coniston Lake affords a greater breadth of motive power and train formations.

Take the re-creation of the 'Lakes Express', which originally served Keswick rather than Coniston, occasionally features prestige 'Princess Coronation' 4-6-2 46238 *City of Carlisle*. The portioned carriages of the train that originated at Euston reverses and continues its journey to the entirely imaginary Coniston Town with local motive power, usually an Ivatt 'Micky Mouse' tank. Meanwhile, the visiting 'Duchess' is turned on shed using the 70ft turntable and serviced prior to taking the return working back to London.

Parallel boiler 'Patriot' 45543 *Home Guard* is occasionally seen on excursion traffic, as is a Carlisle 'Clan'.

Various other exotic locomotives make an appearances, including one of Shap's BR Standard '4MT' bankers, while a Caledonian Railway 0-6-0 sometimes pops-up collecting minerals for Scotland's heavy industry.

Other formations that reflect those seen in Cumbria in the 1960s are represented in the form of block trains of CovHops on the St Helens-Corkickle working and a train of 21 ton coal hoppers, usually powered by Stanier '8Fs' together with trains of iron ore hoppers from the (yes, fictional!) local mines to Barrow and Millom under the power of Ivatt '4MT' 2-6-0 or Fowler '4F' 0-6-0.

"I used to see 'Jubilee' 45606 *Falkland Islands* frequently on an afternoon goods train when at Millom School," the layout's creator recalls and so it is no surprise to see it put in appearances on Coniston Lake on such duties.

"There is no timetable," Mike continues. "I simply enjoy watching the trains go by."

Satisfying extras

Mike's target was to create the illusion of a main line with long sweeping curves was aided by the use of finescale SMP bullhead rail, blended with Marcway points with careful painting and weathering.

Track on the main running lines has superelevation on curved sections to improve the appearance, while authentic variation in colour and texture was »

'8F' 48151 heads south with a string of hopper wagons as Fairburn 2-6-4T 42119 and Stanier 2-6-4T 42581 lift the 'Lakes Express' up the steep incline and over the main line on the branch to Coniston Town.

Above: **Clever trickery of models and photographs makes for an effective town scene. Careful placement of road vehicles also helps disguise the join.**

CONISTON LAKE TRACK DIAGRAM (Not to scale)

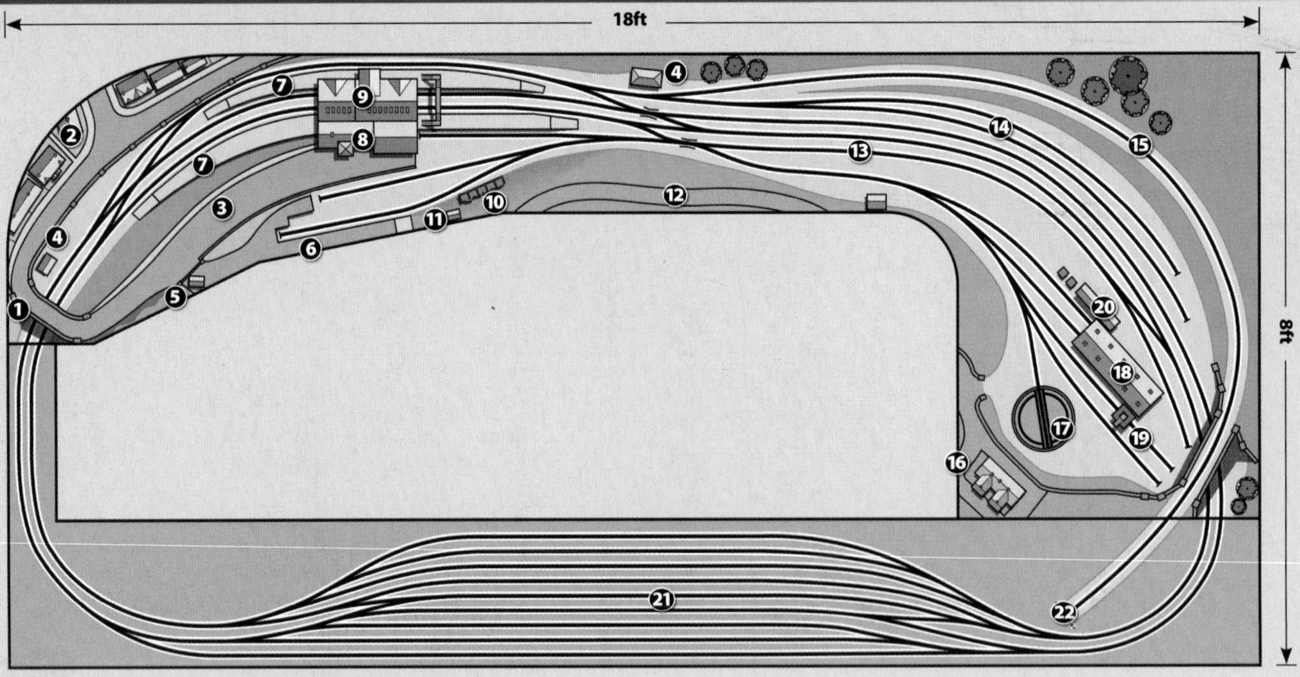

18ft

8ft

KEY

1 Road overbridge	5 Yard office	9 Portico roof	13 Goods loop	17 Turntable	21 Main storage yard
2 Town scene	6 Loading dock	10 Coal staithes	14 Goods sidings	18 Engine shed	22 To high-level storage yard
3 Station approach	7 Platform	11 Coal office	15 Coniston Town branch	19 Coaling tower	
4 Signalbox	8 Station building	12 Road	16 Railway Terrace	20 Stores	

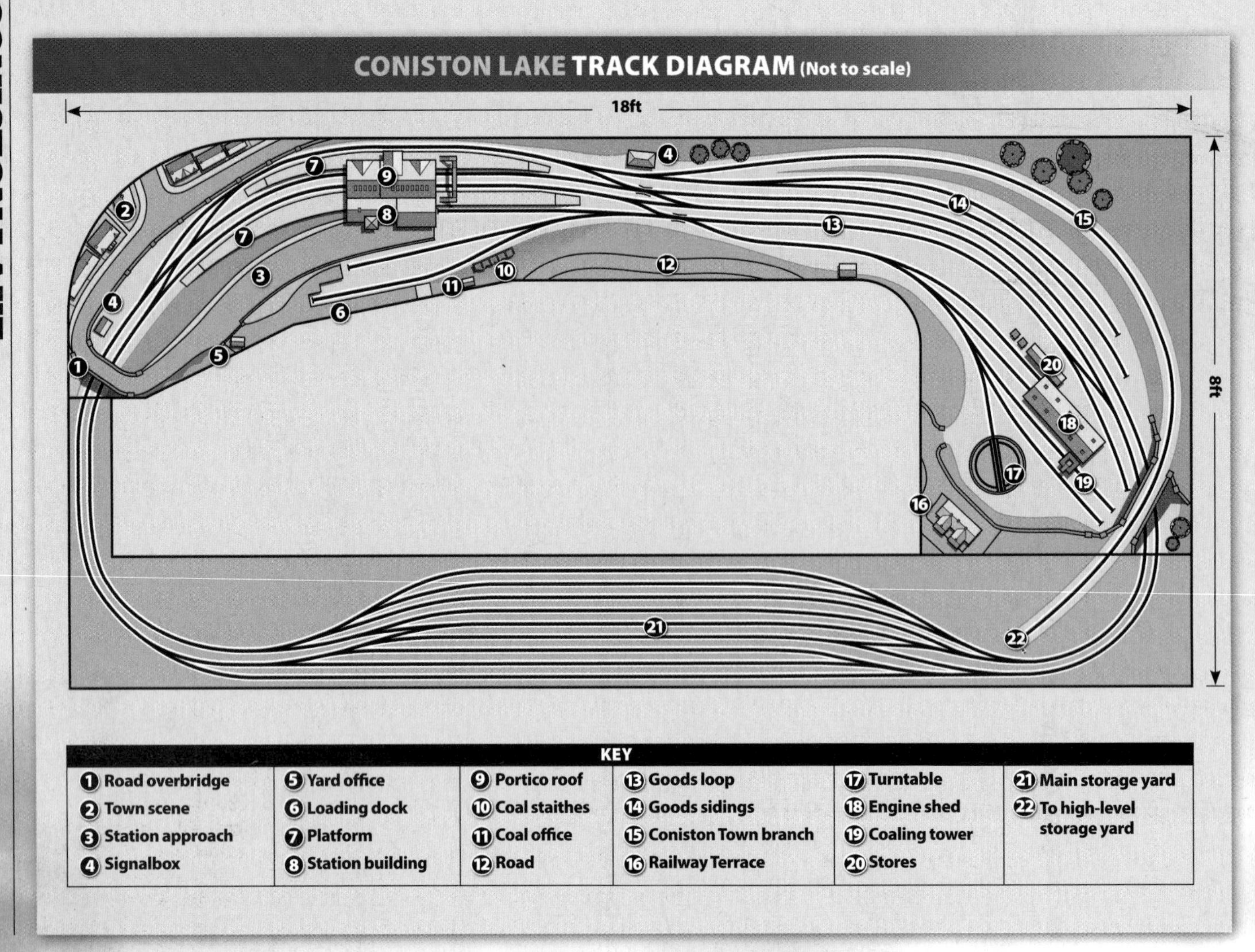

Lord Rowallan rolls into Coniston Lake almost unnoticed with a Travelling Post Office set.

Carnforth-allocated 'Black Five' 44709 'rubs shoulders' with Fowler '4F' 44356. Taking shelter in the cosy confines of the shed is Hughes-Fowler 'Crab' 2-6-0 42789.

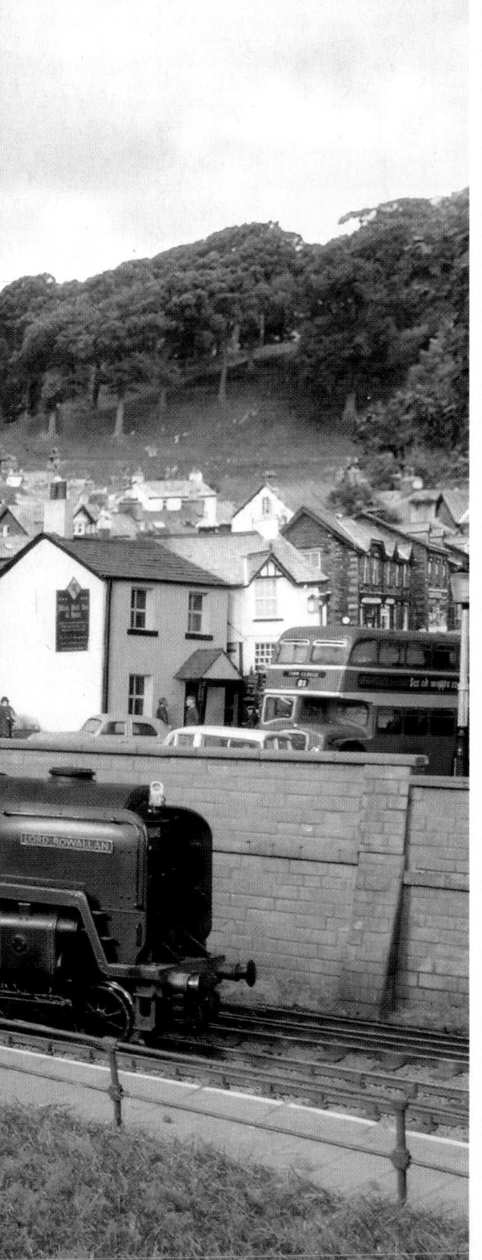

achieved interest by using different ballast where appropriate; fine grey for the main lines and cinders for the sidings.

Semaphore signals function using servo control units are all electrically interlocked with the corresponding points.

"I find the interlocking of points and signals very satisfying and genuinely useful in that I know the road is set if the signal can be cleared," says Mike.

Dummy point rodding adds considerably to the overall appearance.

Scenery is built up using offcuts of art mountboard then covered in Modroc, which is painted a variety of suitable subdued countryside colours and then covered in scenic materials.

This landscape is liberally populated with dry stone walling (created from photographs of the real thing), telegraph poles, fencing, cars and vans, and people.

The backscene of Coniston Water was created from a series of images taken standing on the lakeside and digitally stitched together before being printed as a banner on a commercial printer.

"I was really pleased with the illusion created by the blending of the foreground scenery with the backscene."

The townscape, based on nearby Broughton-in-Furness, was slightly more complicated as "lots of photographs of the town" were "manipulated in various" before printing.

Coniston Lake might look complete, but Mike says that "there is still plenty of detailing to complete, new signals to construct, weathering to improve… the railway will continue to evolve as the years pass." ■

READ MORE

Visit www.keymodelworld.com

A 'stopper' leaves Coniston Lake behind Stanier 4-6-0 45445 parallel to a branch line service with Ivatt '2MT' 46432.

Dragonby

It started life as an all-action slice of the Great Western Main Line in the early 1990s, but now resembles a more generic setting of the privatised 21st Century era. **GEOFF BUTLER** relays how Acton Main Line morphed into Dragonby.

PHOTOGRAPHY, MIKE WILD

IF THE NUMBER of shows attended is a barometer for a layout's popularity, then Dragonby must be one of the most loved in Britain.

This East Midland/North East 'N' gauge magnum opus has racked-up almost 200 appearances on the exhibition circuit since making its debut in three decades ago.

But what you see here is quite different from its inception by Croydon Model Railway Society when it resembled Acton Main Line on the Great Western Main Line

As current owner Geoff Buttler surmises, "at the time 'N' gauge layouts of this calibre were rare on the exhibition circuit and its popularity came about through the builders' attention to detail at the lineside and beyond as well as their fastidiously detailed locomotives and rolling stock".

Acton Main Line's standout feature was its six circuits of continual running, affording the spectacle of multiple trains passing as well as operations taking place in the stone terminal alongside. It was retired in 2004.

Meanwhile, an unfortunate stroke caused Geoff's modelling ability to be "greatly reduced", prompting him to "seek out a reasonable ready built layout" that reflected his desire to run realistic length diesel and electric era train formations not possible in 'OO' with the room available. It was no surprise then that Acton Main Line was readily snapped-up as soon as it was made available by the Croydon group.

Given its hard life on tour, the layout required some restoration, namely replacing a number of Peco point motors and the installation of more than 100 trees; a combination of Woodland Scenics products to give depth and to add subtle changes to the scenery. Static grass was used to give texture to the "very tired" vegetation.

All action

The most striking change was the layout's shift in portrayal from West London to somewhere generically on the eastern side of England "to better suit the privatisation era stock available" and, naturally enough, this called for a new name. Geoff plucked for Dragonby; a small village close to Scunthorpe in his locality, although the layout bears no resemblance to it at all other than there is a railway line that passes the village.

It was exhibited in its new form for the first time in 2006.

However, "the ethos of the layout remains much as before", says Geoff, depicting a busy main line station, with an adjacent freight yard and aggregates/ cement discharge point.

There are four control panels, two of which have two controllers each for the Up and Down fast and slow lines. While there are no points on these tracks, there are isolating sections for each in the off-scene storage yard which can hold at least five trains per track. The third panel again has two controllers, this operating the Up and Down freight lines and the yard with three isolating sections to each line in the fiddle yard. The final panel with one controller serves the goods yard only, but allows two operators to work the yard at the same time.

"Our main aim is to entertain the public and keep things moving."

GEOFF BUTTLER

We added working colour signals by what are now marketed under the Absolute Aspects banner. These are operated by rotary switches.

With all this potential activity, Dragonby requires four operators to perform efficiently at exhibitions.

"Our main aim is to entertain the public and keep things moving, which generally happens thanks to the robust track and the improved performance and reliability of current locomotives and rolling stock."

This results in the ability to put on an "intensive timetable with no waiting for train movements". »

'N' at its breath-taking best. A CrossCountry Voyager heads away from the camera towards the station. Heading the other way is GBRf Construction-liveried Class 66 66793 (a custom repaint), hauling Castle Cement tanks, just as a Class 60 draws a rake of HOA hoppers out of the aggregates' terminal.

Graffiti and weed-infested trackside infrastructure reflects the warts-and-all nature of Dragonby's contemporary depiction of the railway today. A Freightliner Class 66 with a rake of MJA wagons crosses paths with the Network Rail NMT emerging from the fiddle yard.

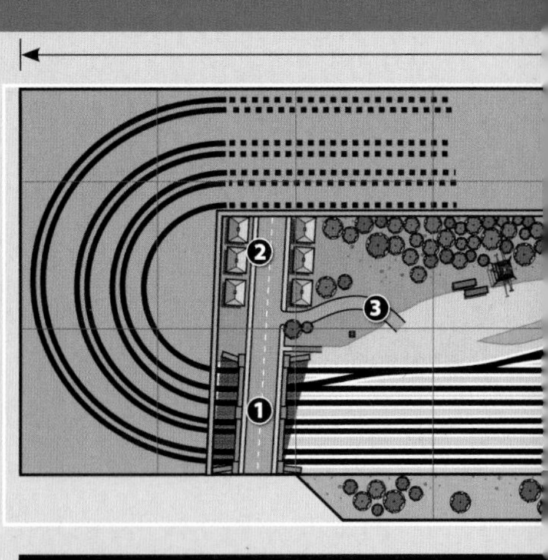

1. Road overbridge
2. Houses
3. Yard access road

The subtle, yet highly effective, cambering of the curves adds to the realism, particularly when a High Speed Train leans intothem. This effect was originally achieved by inserting various thickness of plasticard from beneath the track centres to the outside of the curve and a section of the approach straight so that rolling stock has a smooth run through the canted section.

Outstanding mix

Few would disagree with Geoff's sentiment that the standard of 'N' gauge models these days is "outstanding", which contributes significantly to Dragonby's success.

As you might imagine, there is a huge amount of stock required to operate the layout with classes including 37, 47, 56, 57, 58, 60, 66, 67, 68 and 70s. Many of these have received one off repaints to replicate specific locomotives including GBRf Class 66s.

Second generation DMUs are also much in evidence with classes 150, 153, 156, 158 and 170 all of which are fitted with Tomix working Dellner couplings at the cab ends. This allows the Bachmann Class 158 to be coupled to the Dapol Class 153s and 156s.

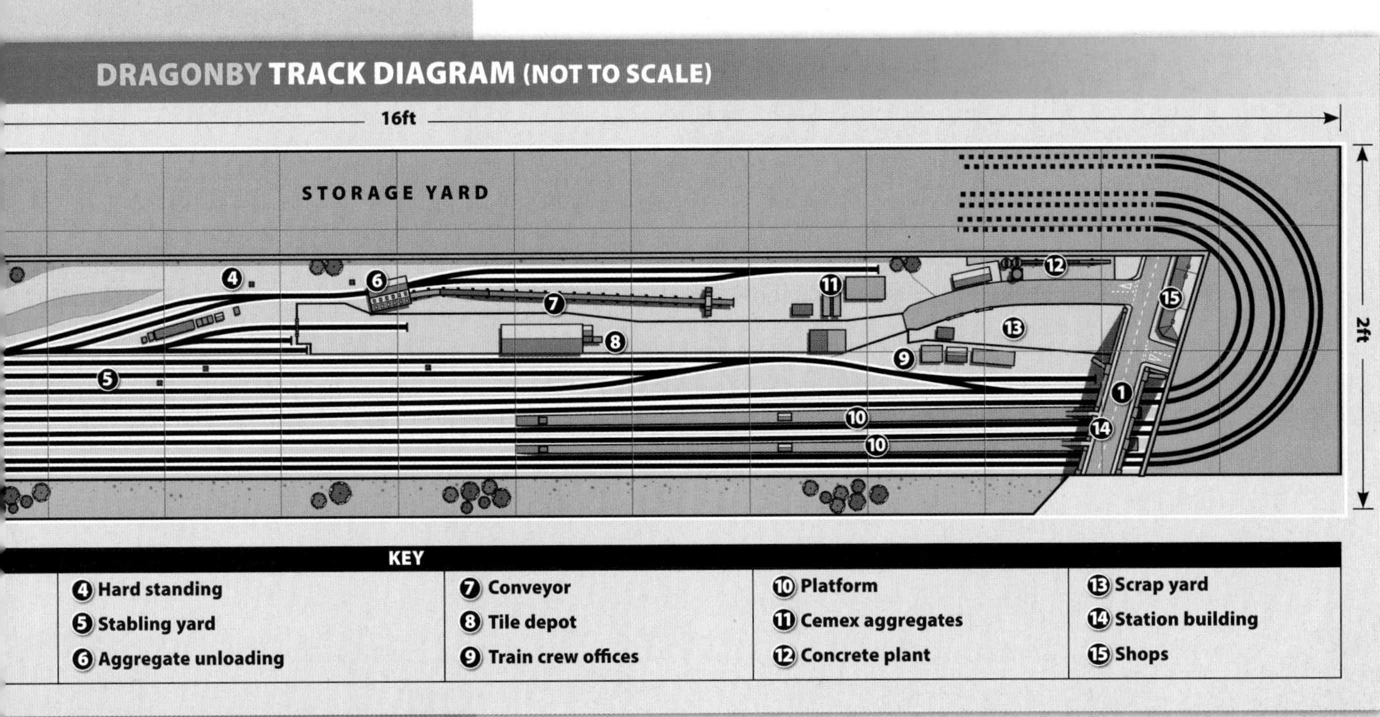

Rounding things off are Voyagers in Virgin and CrossCountry colours along with a number of HST sets and a Virgin Trains Class 390 Pendolino.

On the freight side, there are 350 or so wagons (some 3D printed for variety) with 99% of the stock weathered to some degree.

Conscious that he and his helpers "are not getting any younger", Geoff's relays that Dragonby's exhibition dates in the near future may be its last and so his message is to enjoy it "while you can". ■

Below: **Such is the quality of workmanship and off-the-shelf rolling stock that, at first glance, you could imagine this is 'OO' gauge. Class 70 70003 powers a cement train parallel Class 37/4 37409 with a DRS nuclear train while passenger services are provided by Class 220 and 156 multiple units.**

READ MORE

Visit www.keymodelworld.com

Below: **Anyone who knows Acton Main Line might spot the Dragonby's prototype provenance with all of its buildings dating back to the layout's original construction. Class 66 66222 powers under the road bridge at Dragonby with a rake of IZA Cargowaggon twins as a 'Pacer' shudders to a halt in the platforms.**

SHOP

- Limited editions
- Exclusive products
- Modelling essentials

KEY PUBLISHING LIMITED EDITIONS!

DCC READY 40145 - IN STOCK NOW!
DCC SOUND FITTED 40145 - PRE-ORDER NOW!

Bachmann Class 40 40145 *East Lancashire Railway* in BR large logo blue for 'OO' gauge.

£229.95 DCC ready

£329.95 DCC sound fitted

- Updated tooling
- Choice of DCC ready and DCC sound fitted
- Highly detailed
- Etched metal nameplates
- Limited to 500 models

Pre-order now with a £10 deposit – due September 2023

PRE-ORDER NOW! Accurascale Class 31 31276 *Calder Hall Power Station* in Railfreight Coal Sector livery for 'OO' gauge

- Brand-new tooling
- Choice of DCC ready and DCC sound fitted
- Highly detailed
- Etched metal nameplates
- Limited to 300 models

£169.99 DCC ready

SOLD OUT DCC sound fitted

Pre-order now with a £10 deposit – due early 2024

IN STOCK NOW!

'OO' GAUGE DIESEL BRAKE TENDERS

B964040E in BR green

£36.99

LAST FEW REMAINING!

B964113 in BR green with small yellow warning panels, weathered

£38.99

£36.99

B964066E in BR green with small yellow warning panels

please visit...

.com/shop

DENT

Recreating Britain's highest main line station in 'OO' provided welcome relief from the pressures of the pandemic for NHS manager **NICK CASON**.

PHOTOGRAPHY, MIKE WILD

POPULARITY OF model railways mushroomed during the first pandemic lockdown as millions across nation suddenly had oodles of free time on their hands. For Nick Cason, the reality was quite different, but the therapy that modelling brought was just as valuable, if not more so.

"As a paramedic general manager with the Ambulance Service based in Norwich, I have found that the longer days, and busy on calls that supporting the pandemic response can bring, require equal downtime to unwind," he says. "And what better way to do it than recreating a bit of history in an area I love?

"I have had a lifelong interest in railways but with no particular allegiance to region or period. I have modelled in 'OO' and 'N' and have never completed a project before another comes along. However, I do also enjoy fell running and hiking, and I found quite easily that spending time around the Settle – Carlisle allowed me to enjoy both at the same time.

"Dent fascinates me – a station that even in 2021 has almost nobody living within an easy walk of it. The main road up to it is as steep as they come and after descending it, the view uphill to the railway is quite exceptional – how many places on the rail network can you be so far beneath a main line railway running along the contours of somewhere like Dentdale?"

"Dent fascinates me – a station that even in 2021 has almost nobody living within an easy walk of it."

Building blocks

The result of all that inspiration is a miniature tribute to Dent… in a Norfolk garden shed.

As well as the impressive landscape, the original Midland Railway-era track layout England's highest mainline station "has a lot »

A whopping coal train follows '9F' 92185 north through Dent, 1,150ft above sea level, which in 'OO' model model terms would be about 15ft.

to offer" from a modelling perspective with no facing points, two slips, a short dock siding, and layby sidings for the Up and Down lines.

The majority of this was recreated with Peco's Code 75 bullhead track except for the slips, which weren't in production at the time of Nick's build.

Building wise, the platforms are relatively short and therefore easy to model at scale length. The key station buildings are offered by Hornby's Skaledale range; the main station building, waiting room, signalbox and snowsheds.

Plans for the famous 1-in-10 Coal Road bridge required more thought. The original 1875 are reproduced in *Stations and*

Realistic trains in breath-taking surrounds.

Structures of the Settle and Carlisle Railway, allowing Nick to scratchbuild it using a foamboard core covered in brick sheeting. Arches cut from the Wills retaining arches kit were ideal for three of the four arches, but the larger one spanning the double track required individual brick scribing using plasticard.

Other than the necessary painting and weathering with acrylics, the finishing touch is provided with the addition of the white signal sighting board for the Down 'starter'.

The platforms are also scratchbuilt from a foamboard base, topped with card and a Polyfilla surface. The edging stones are scribed from plasticard and painted to give the impression of individually laid stones.

Horsebox to cattle van, via the dock.

A parcels train (including a couple of horseboxes) runs non-stop through Dent behind 'Royal Scot' 46120 *Royal Inniskilling Fusilier*. Rise Hill Tunnel has been moved a few miles south to provide a natural scenic break behind the Coal Road bridge.

The retaining walls are made from Wills stone sheets, although the curved ones could only be formed after some time in the oven!

The Wills stone viaduct kit played a key part in the representation of Dent Head viaduct, with prototypical parapet walls added.

There is three miles between Rise Hill and Blea Moor tunnels either side of Dent and so some creative compression was required so that they could be used as the natural scenic breaks. The ever-present Peco tunnel mouth mouldings made the ideal portals.

Random Rock

Constructing a layout in a garden shed can be problematic with fluctuations in temperature, but thanks to input from Nick's father and father-in-law, Dent's home was lined, lit and heated from the start.

The most significant shift from the plan was to bring the out and back loops inside from their original covered lean-to-shelters, which weren't pleasant to access in the cold. The shed was therefore extended to 25ft long, remaining at 12ft wide, bringing everything indoors.

This size allowed for a "decent fiddle yard" of 18 sidings, flanked by scissor crossovers allowing for Up and Down trains to be prototypically interchanged. "This was a difficult decision", says Nick, "as putting these in takes up room that reduces the yard length," although the longest siding can still accommodate a '9F' and 45 four-wheel wagons.

Dent is based around standard baseboard construction: 75mmx25mm frame with 6mm ply over the trackbed and open-top where the scenery dips below track level.

The main scenic base is built up from Plaster of Paris bandages set over a lattice cardboard frame ("a very therapeutic pastime"), with layers of Woodland Scenics' scatters, with trees built-up from Noch seafoam, with scatter affixed with cheap hairspray.

As well as end-to-end, Nick also had to "play around" with the front-to-back as he "needed the valley to rise behind the viaduct more steeply than in reality so that it could meet the backscene and not be wide open". »

A filthy 'Dub Dee' clanks south over Dent Head Viaduct and into Blea Moor Tunnel.

"To that end I put in a cliff wall (with climbers), made from plaster poured into a multi-layered tin foil mould. Using six-seven layers of tin foil glued together makes a decent and strong enough mould box.

"Screwing this up forms random rock cracks and placing a ruler across those in parallel gives an indication of strata. Once dried it was painted with acrylic paints and given a light dusting with an airbrush."

The representation of Monkey Beck, immediately to the north of the station, was made with a Polyfilla covering, sealed with PVA glue, painted using earthly colour and sand/pebbles added before three layers of Deluxe Materials Aqua Magic was drizzled over.

Matchsticks stuck side-by-side onto lollipops were used to represent the lengthy runs of snow fencing above track level.

Class 40 D368 passes through with a long train of vans.

Leeds Holbeck-allocated 'Jubilee' 45659 *Drake* rushes through with a Carlisle-bound express.

As if that wasn't creative enough, a technique was borrowed from Colin Fisher's Mossdale (HM145) that uses cat litter for drystone walls.

"In essence it was a mix of non-absorbent cat litter (sieved using the kitchen cheese grater), black powder paint, PVA, plaster and water," Nick explains. "Give it all a mix, hope for the best and place with childrens' glue applicators."

Ballast is a mix of colours to indicate patching, and grade changes for the sidings, all weathered with an airbrush.

Slowly upgrading

Control is DCC using three NCE Power Cab handheld units, while points are switched by analogue control across two control boards »

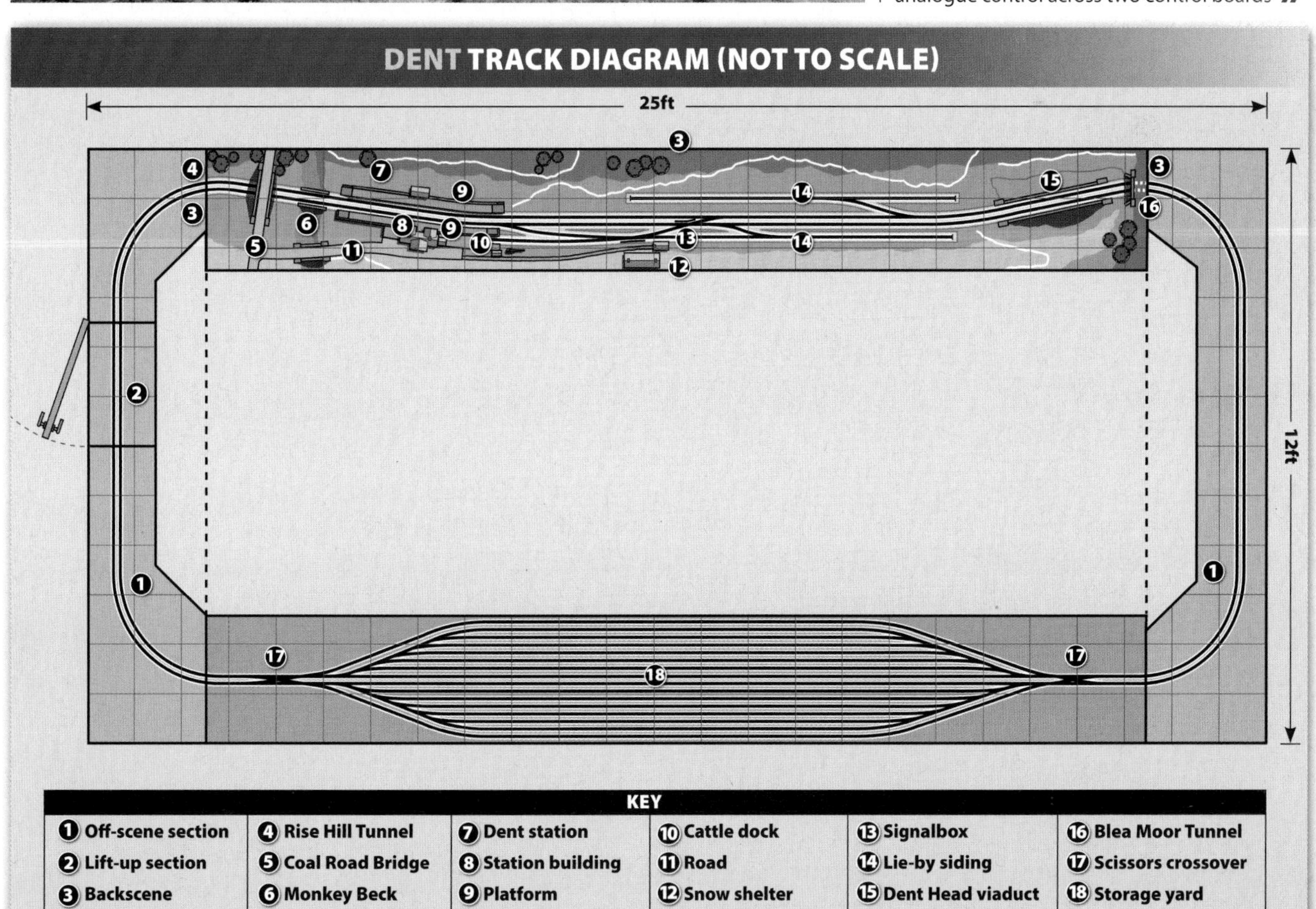

DENT TRACK DIAGRAM (NOT TO SCALE)

25ft

12ft

KEY

1 Off-scene section	4 Rise Hill Tunnel	7 Dent station	10 Cattle dock	13 Signalbox	16 Blea Moor Tunnel
2 Lift-up section	5 Coal Road Bridge	8 Station building	11 Road	14 Lie-by siding	17 Scissors crossover
3 Backscene	6 Monkey Beck	9 Platform	12 Snow shelter	15 Dent Head viaduct	18 Storage yard

Derby Lightweight DMUs cross for the measly number of passengers who use the station serving the village five miles away.

Above: **Backbreaking work for the poor man emptying this 16-ton mineral wagon of coal.**

Below: **This LNWR 'Super D' must be on a diversionary working from the West Coast Main Line, crossing paths with a '9F' which is a much more familiar sight for the 'S&C'.**

(Tortoise and Cobalt on the scenic section and Peco surface mounts on the fiddle yard).

Most of the motive power fleet is steam in BR black late crest livery, including classes '3F', '4F', 'WD', '9F', 'Jubilee' and 'Royal Scot', with green diesels that were also regulars to the 'S&C', such as '25', '40', '45' and '47'.

Work in progress is slowly upgrading locomotives to sound and experimenting with variations of chips and speakers: "I have to say that I love iPhone speakers for size, ease of installation and quality of sound", Nick says.

All stock will eventually be weathered too.

Nick signs-off with a word for his "very supportive wife for letting me spend evenings in the shed and helping on some of them", as well as his children Tom and Eleanor "or showing enough interest in its building and running to back its continuation".

"It's an incredibly relaxing pastime that can include the whole family." ■

READ MORE

Visit www.keymodelworld.com

VISIT OUR ONLINE SHOP

TO VIEW OUR FULL RANGE OF **RAIL BOOKS**

KEY Shop

shop.keypublishing.com/books

NEW

CLASS 57s
MARK V. PIKE

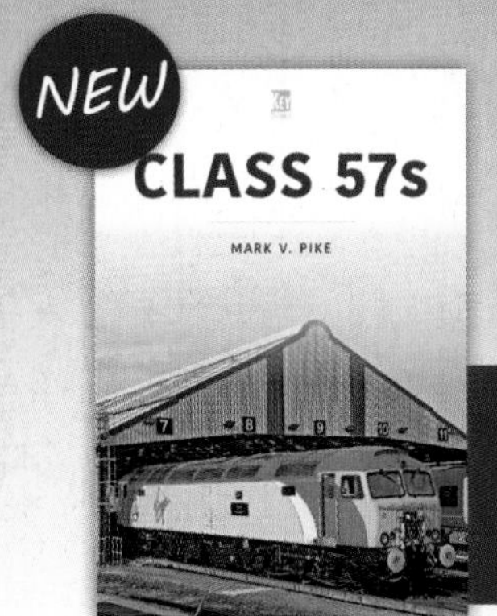

Known irreverently as 'bodysnatchers', the Class 57s have filled a gap in available traction for the last two decades and the fleet is intact today, continuing to see use with various TOCs and future-proofed by overhaul. All 33 locos are depicted in this volume, with over 200 images in number order from 57001–57012, 57301–57316 and 57601–57605, showing a variety of duties with which they have been entrusted in the last 20 years.

ONLY £16·99

SUBSCRIBERS don't forget to use your **£2 OFF DISCOUNT CODE!**

CLASS 31s
MARK V. PIKE

Perhaps overshadowed by more 'exotic' locos, the Class 31s nonetheless played a significant part in British Railways' Modernisation Plan.

This volume includes more than 200 images showing these workhorses in action, mostly in the south of England.

ONLY £16·99

SUBSCRIBERS don't forget to use your **£2 OFF DISCOUNT CODE!**

RAIL FREIGHT
LONDON AND THE SOUTH EAST

PAUL SHANNON

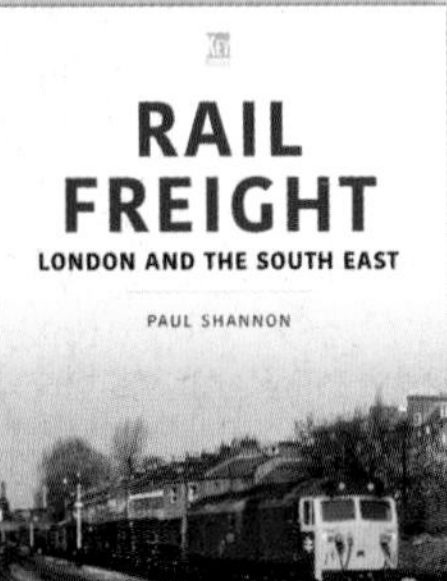

Illustrated with more than 160 photographs, many of which are previously unpublished, this volume looks at the changing face of rail freight in London and the South East of England. It details the transformation in traction, rolling stock and railway infrastructure over four decades.

ONLY £16·99

SUBSCRIBERS don't forget to use your **£2 OFF DISCOUNT CODE!**

ELECTROSTAR
CAPITAL COMMUTER

IAN BUCK

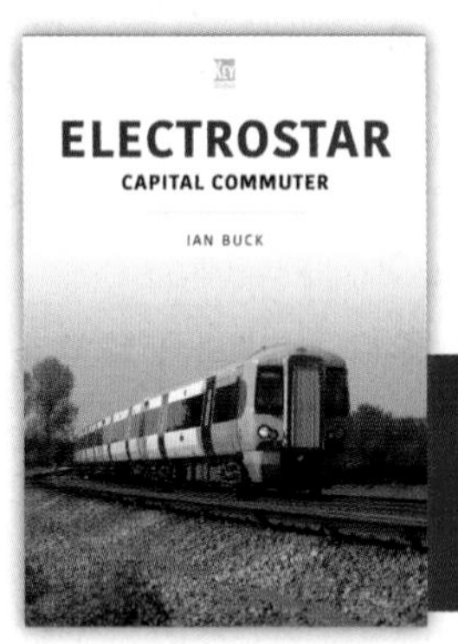

With nearly 200 previously unpublished images, this book gives an overview of the routes the Electrostar has worked, or is still working, as well as the different companies that these unsung heroes of the everyday railway have served.

ONLY £15·99

SUBSCRIBERS don't forget to use your **£2 OFF DISCOUNT CODE!**

LONDON UNDERGROUND
THE NORTHERN LINE

JONATHAN JAMES

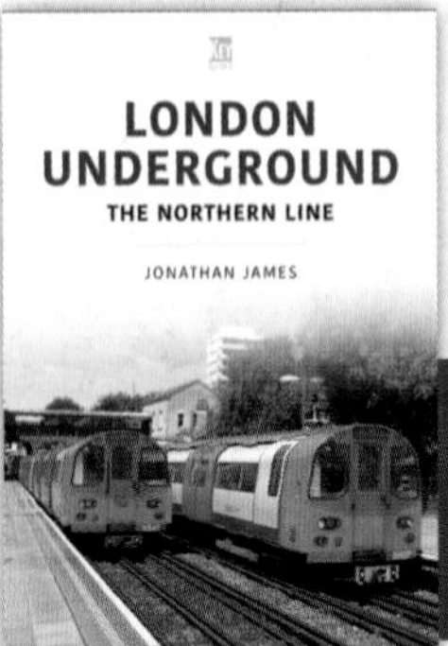

This book charts the progression of the Northern line, which dates back more than 125 years, and illustrates how three railway companies evolved and then merged to become one vast operation integrated into London's transport system.

ONLY £17·99

SUBSCRIBERS don't forget to use your **£2 OFF DISCOUNT CODE!**

HERITAGE DMUs
THE FINAL YEARS

IAN BUCK

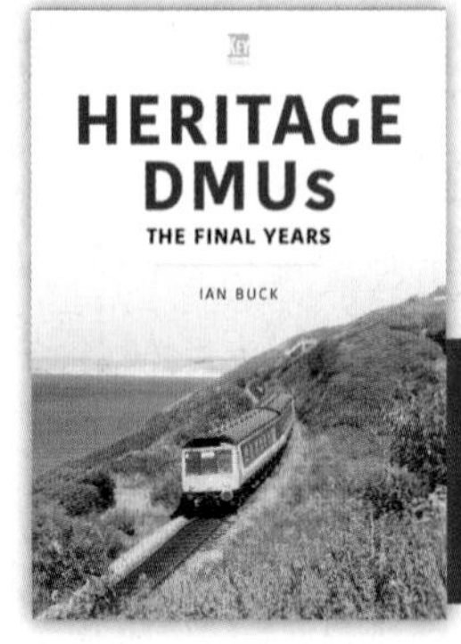

This book provides an overview of the final operations that the heritage DMUs were involved in. These unsung heroes of the 1955 modernisation plan certainly gave their worth and, thankfully, many can still be seen today on the railway preservation scene.

ONLY £16·99

SUBSCRIBERS don't forget to use your **£2 OFF DISCOUNT CODE!**

CLASS 68s
ANDY FLOWERS

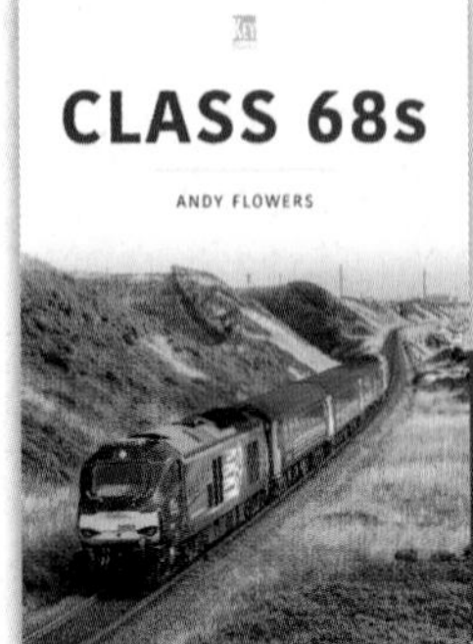

A detailed technical specification is included in this book, together with a review of DRS's chartered services of recent years, including on railtours. Illustrated with more than 100 photographs, this visual guide presents a comprehensive overview of the role of today's Class 68.

ONLY £16·99

SUBSCRIBERS don't forget to use your **£2 OFF DISCOUNT CODE!**

BRITISH RAIL SHUNTERS
THE FINAL YEARS

SIMON BENDALL

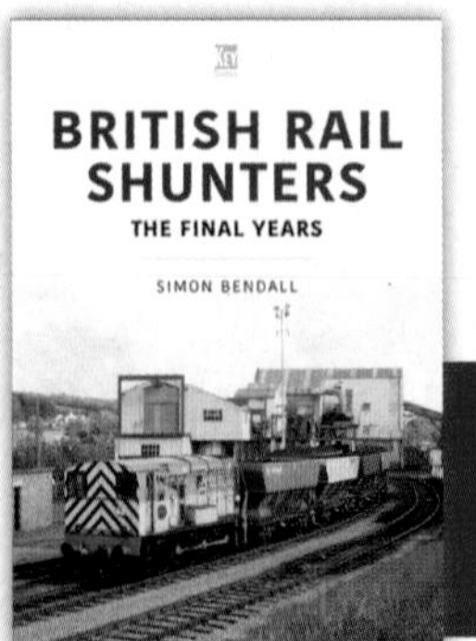

This book delves into a period of substantial reorganisation with a pictorial look at the shunter fleet in its final years of BR ownership between 1990 and 1996, tracing the changes in operators, the emergence of new colour schemes and alterations in deployment.

ONLY £16·99

SUBSCRIBERS don't forget to use your **£2 OFF DISCOUNT CODE!**

FREE P&P* when you order online at...

shop.keypublishing.com/books

Call +44 (0)1780 480404 *(Monday to Friday 9am-5.30pm GMT)*

**Free 2nd class P&P on all UK & BFPO orders. Overseas charges apply.*

503/23

Little Burford

Making the best of available space is key to a successful layout even if it means making compromises, as **DAN EVASON** discovered when he ventured into 'O' gauge for the first time.

PHOTOGRAPHY, MIKE WILD

Collett 'Tanner One-er' 6110 brings an assortment of 'GW' wagons into Little Burford station. Rather than being parallel to the baseboard edge, the main line leaves the baseboard at an angle along with the coal siding tailing off in the opposite direction to add visual interest.

"AN IMPORTANT lesson is that even experienced layout builders can overestimate the amount of space they have when drawing a layout on paper," says professional modelmaker Dan Evason. "Sometimes, only when you start building the layout do limitations become apparent."

Such considerations were vital in the decision making that led to the construction of Little Burford in 7mm:1ft. This 'O' gauge gem reflects a desire for its commissioning owner Mike Hickling "to capture the timeless rural sleepy station atmosphere of the 1930s… a time where there was great pride in 'the station' with its well-maintained buildings and flower beds by its small group of station staff".

As originally set out by Dan and Mike ("over a packet of biscuits and a cuppa"), the GWR county branch line set piece was intended to be hooked-up to a circuit in the latter's double-garage when not being exhibited at shows.

Practical constraints defeated such an idea, especially given the space guzzling 'OO' gauge layout running around the perimeter of the room. Instead, Little Burford evolved to sit on trestles in the middle of it.

The 4ft x 14in baseboards (with 3ft long traversers at each end) were bolted together, and a fiddle yard added to the area at the back as an afterthought, with tracks linking to both traversers to make the layout more enjoyable to run. One has two storage lines, adding to flexibility.

In essence however, this is a "very simplistic plan" comprising a passing loop and two sidings on the scenic side.

This makes it ideal for one-man operation, but in order to keep things continuously moving »

How's that for detail? The signalman watches the slow pace of a branch line take its course from the steps of his signal box, of which we're given a teasing glimpse inside.

No room is left un-detailed!

at exhibitions, two operators are required: one to drive the trains and the other operate the signalling as well as coupling trains.

What Little Burford lacks in complexity is made up by "all the little aspects" which Dan considers "a treat for the eyes".

Having previously modelling in scales no bigger than 4mm:1ft, working with this larger scale means that "detail is even more important, with everything having to be considered carefully."

This means signal wires, 'damaged' downpipes and cow pats in the cattle dock make all the difference. There are even legible notices inside the coal office; one notice cheekily reads 'Little Burford – built by Dan Evason'.

'O' off the shelf

'O' gauge infrastructure has historically been the preserve of scratch builders, but advances in the ready-to-run trade means that there are plenty of high-quality proprietary items on view.

The signal box is a laser cut Peco kit, with an additional interior detailing kit (with telegraph communications provided by a run of Peco 'poles'). Visible through its large sliding windows is a stove, kettle and chair for the Modelu signalman to rest in once he has finished leaning from his staircase.

In fact, all the figures on Little Burford are 3D-printed Modelu items, "which really bring the layout to life", together with the plug-and-lay Woodland Scenics lighting.

Laser Cut Model Railway Kits provided the dainty station building and waiting shelter. Peer inside the ticket office and you will see a porter having a quiet brew near to the cosy fireplace, albeit dormant in this summer scene.

Dapol semaphore signals protect train operations together with ground signals from Invertrains, Dunfermline. The Dapol lower quadrants operate via switches mounted to the control box with DCC Concepts S levers for ease of operation.

The control panel can be clipped on to the front or rear of the layout depending whether it is at home or at an exhibition and needs to be operated from the rear.

"I was even dipping in and out of the workshop on Christmas Day."

DAN EVASON

Dapol again comes into its own for the key items of ready-to-go motive power and rolling stock.

The archetypal GWR branch line train comes from the Chirk-based manufacturer in the form of its Collett '48XX' 0-4-2T and Churchward autotrailer. A '43XX' 2-6-0 "stretches the size envelope but does look great running complete with DCC sound".

Dan adds that his favourite rolling stock are the six-wheel milk tankers "which really stand out with their royal blue livery against the largely grey GWR freight stock".

Scenic journey

As a country setting, scenery plays as much of a part of the layout's successful execution as the buildings and trains.

Open meadows are made from World War Scenics materials, with good old hanging basket liner used as an underlay for static grass.

Although the principles of scenic modelling are largely the same as any other gauge Dan has worked with, he discovered that building the layout in winter meant that the ballast took a week to dry. "I was even dipping in and out of the workshop on Christmas Day trying help the drying procedure with the wife's hair dryer!"

Not that has put him off 'O' gauge.

"I really want to build myself a small layout in the scale," he resolves. "It really is lovely to work in and with increasing amounts of ready-to-run models available is becoming increasingly accessible." ■

READ MORE

Visit www.keymodelworld.com

Below: **Careful colour blending and placement of features of interest means '64XX' pannier tank 6412 rolls past almost unnoticed on its approach to Little Burford.**

LITTLE BURFORD TRACK DIAGRAM (NOT TO SCALE)

KEY

1 To traverser	4 Backscene	7 Platform	10 Track
2 Cattle dock	5 Signalbox	8 Waiting shelter	11 Coal office and yard
3 Hidden storage track	6 Goods loop	9 Station building	12 Road overbridge

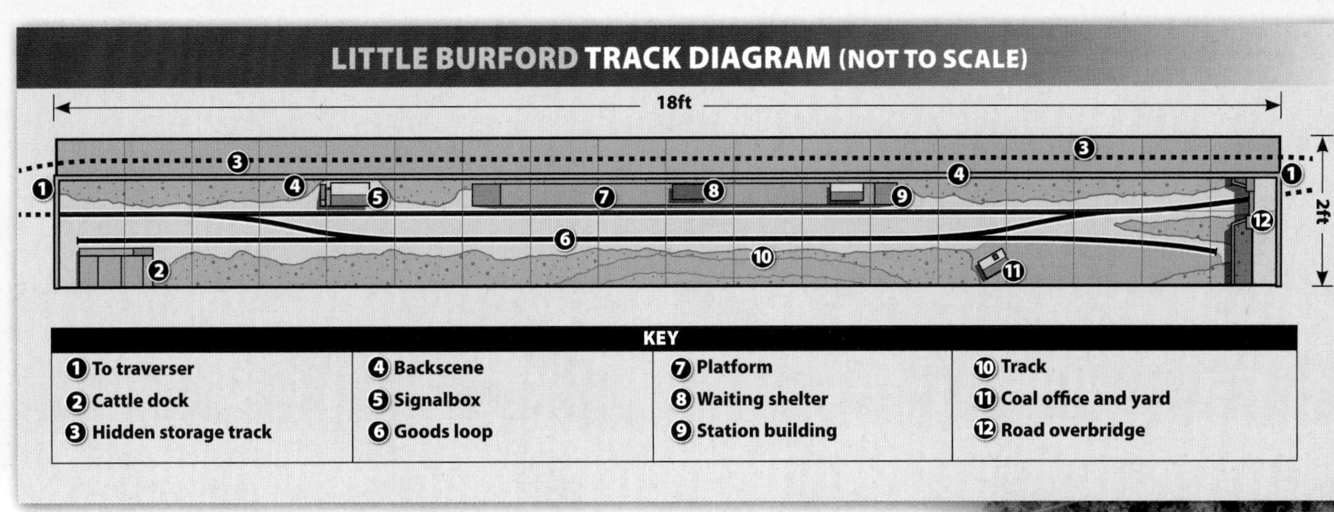

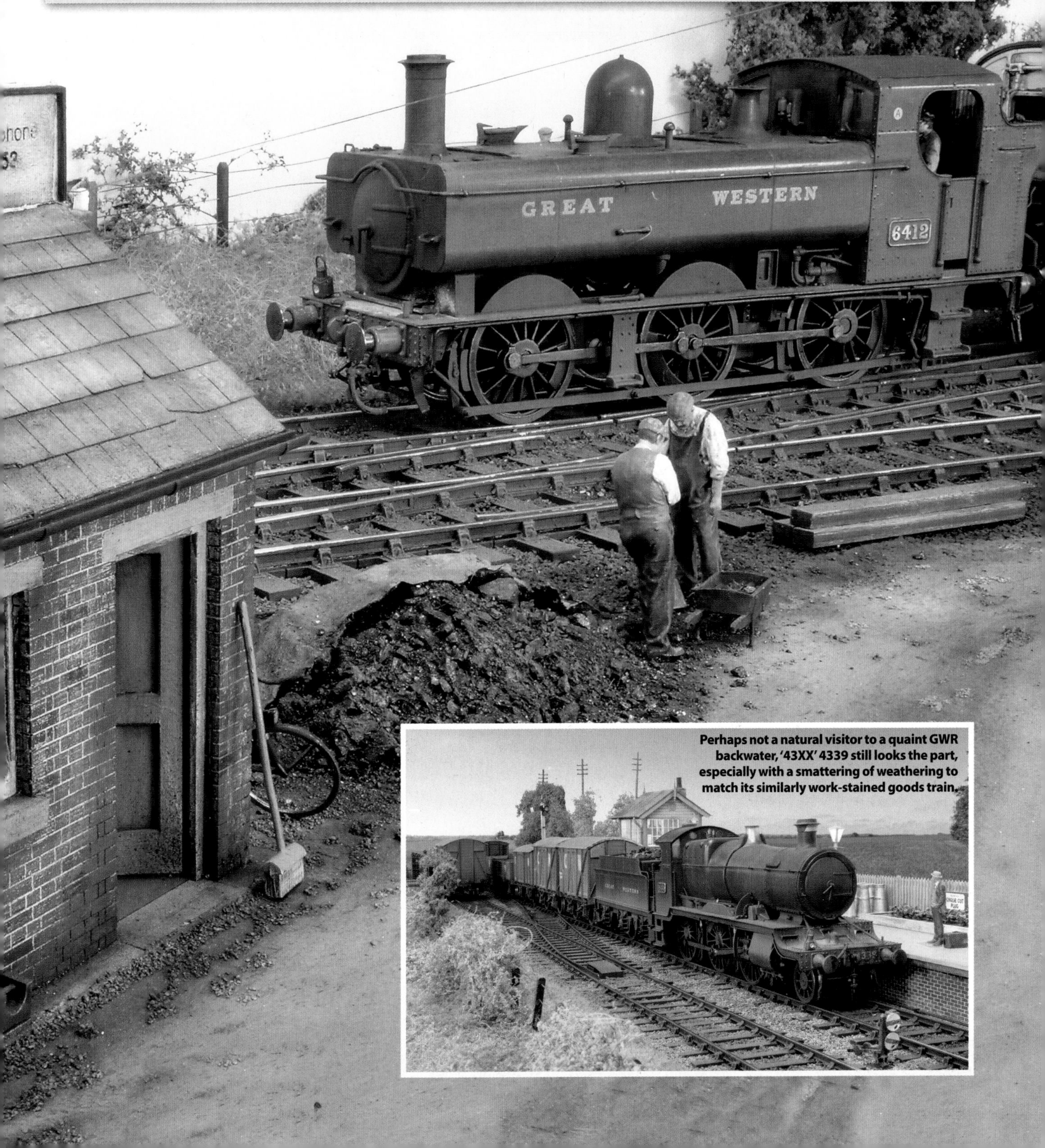

Perhaps not a natural visitor to a quaint GWR backwater, '43XX' 4339 still looks the part, especially with a smattering of weathering to match its similarly work-stained goods train.

Rossiter *Rise*

Red panniers metaphorically rubbing shoulders with EMUs… It can only be pre-1971 London. **TERRY TEW** showcases his latest urban cameo layout creation.

PHOTOGRAPHY, MIKE WILD

THE CAPITAL'S railways make for fascinating modelling topics. Rossiter Rise plays to those strengths, combining two classic themes, yet seldom recreated in layout form.

Having already exhibited his previous layout Earl's Court almost 50 times, Terry Tew was eager to make good use of his fleet North London Line/Euston – Watford EMUs, as well as a newly expanding range of London Transport rolling stock.

The realisation of his ambition, and four years' work, is a busy and compact slice of 'somewhere' in west/north west London in the 1950s.

At the front of the main scenic section is a small LT depot with two tracks leading into a workshop, plus a headshunt leading to a single road steam shed. Directly behind this is a dead-end London Underground bay platform.

This meets a pair of through four-rail DC lines in the style of the North London Line, plus a another through, non-electrified platform at the rear.

The layout consists of a main scenic section placed centrally with a traverser/fiddle yard to the left and a fiddle yard to the right. The latter has scenic interest with the interior of the LT works portrayed, visible through 'viewing panel' apertures cut into the fiddle yard screen.

"This adds additional interest rather than just a blank board covering unseen stock," says Terry. "With the opposing traverser/fiddle yard also visible behind the operator at the front of the layout this means there is something for the punters to see along practically the whole length of the layout."

The main 'cameo' scenic baseboard and fiddle yard is homemade while the off-stage traverser is a kit.

The epitome of Rossiter Rise: a London Underground 'Q Stock' unit enters Platform 1 as a Class 501 heads for Willesden. The scratch-built street scene is based on the once notorious Rillington Place.

Lighting is provided by a mixture of 'daylight' bulbs controlled by a dimmer switch and LED strips with controllable colour, hue and brightness, providing maximum control whatever the exhibition surrounds.

P-way and S&T

Vital to the layout's success is its successful portrayal of third/fourth rail permanent way and signal & telegraph infrastructure.

Terry says that a "lot of time" was spent detailing the LT track in particular, including associated cables and timber blocks. A 3D printed 'pig's ear' colour light signal protects the LT yard, while an equally unusual LMS colour light has been scratch built for the representation of the North London Line. A more common LMS semaphore (by Dapol) controls movements from the non-electrified through line.

Rossiter Rise is DCC operated (with the majority of motive power sound fitted) and designed to be run by two operators; one at the front and one at the back. One operator controls the LT depot and bay platform from the front while the rear operator controls all the main line movements.

"We endeavour to keep stock moving!" remarks Terry, pinpointing another of the layout's popular facets.

Eclectic stock

The continuous movements is matched by the variety of motive power and stock on show, effectively separated into four groups.

On the electrified main lines, there are appearances by a three-car LNWR 'Oerlikon unit' (3D printed bodies on propriety chassis); three-car LMS unit (modified Airfix/Dapol suburban coaches); and a three-car 1957 BR '501' unit (modified from a Bachmann '2-EPB').

The non-electrified track sees passenger trains served by three-car 'BUTs'/'ACVs' (3D printed bodies with Heljan railbus driving chassis); pull-push fitted Ivatt 2-6-2T (Bachmann with modified Airfix/Dapol coaches); and an LNWR »

Peering into the 'forced perspective' car garage.

Webb 2-4-2T (kit-built). Goods and parcel workings are handled by Class 15 and 16 diesels (Heljan), '2MT' 2-6-0 and Class 24 (Bachmann).

The LT depot is populated by typically eclectic stock: a Metropolitan Railway 'F' 0-6-2T (kit-built body on propriety chassis); a District Railway 0-6-0T (detailed 3D-printed body on propriety chassis); 'Wheel Carrier' and Ballast Driver (both Radley Models); two battery 'Slug' locomotives (ex-Harrow Model Shop); '57XX' pannier tanks (Bachmann); and 'Met' Bo-Bo electric (Heljan).

Finally, the LT shuttle service is provided by a two-car car 'Standard Stock' unit based on examples that ran over the Northern City Line (Radley Models); and a two-car 'Q Stock' unit (detailed Radley Models).

> *"What something looks like in one's mind can be very different to what it looks like in real life."*
>
> **TERRY TEW**

Buildings

As well as the track and trains, a defining feature of Rossiter Rise is its built-up urban nature. The station is a typically hemmed-in London situation, surrounded retaining and tunnel walls, houses and industrial buildings, developed with a blend of scratch-builds, kits and ready-to-use resin models.

"My philosophy when creating a model is to collect numerous photographs of the various constituent parts and use these as inspiration, paying particular attention to colour and texture," Terry explains. "What something looks like in one's mind can be very different to what it looks like in real life."

This method was used to particularly strong effect in making the row of terraces along the rear of the layout which take their inspiration from Rillington Place in Notting Hill, the location of the notorious Christie

A post-war block of flats overlooks the typically LNWR style station.

ROSSITER RISE TRACK DIAGRAM (NOT TO SCALE)

4ft | 4ft 6in | 4ft | 2ft 8in

KEY			
1 Storage yard	4 London Transport line	7 Terrace houses	10 Canopy
2 London Transport steam shed	5 Water tower	8 Flats	11 Station building
3 Coal stage	6 Signalbox	9 Platform	12 London Transport works

Murders, resulting in a vast amount of film and stills for Terry to based authentic resin castings on.

These and other buildings against the backscene have been arranged in such a way that obvious thin, low relief is avoided, such as pitched rooves sloping up and away from the viewer, rather than side-on.

The imposing block of flats is from the Skytrex range and located on an angle in the right rear corner. In the opposite corner, a small cameo including a partly hidden London bus helps to create an illusion of depth.

This illusion is further enhanced with another cameo, tucked at the rear of the layout: an open industrial doorway through which can be viewed an engineering works. This is actually a small box with hangs on the outside of the backscene, created using 'forced perspective' to trick the eye.

"The exhibition visitors that spot it are often confused by how it's done," says Terry, "and some have been invited around the back of the layout to see for themselves."

The station building utilises proprietary LNWR parts (now available via Peco) and the roof is scratch-built, being based on the one which existed at Belmont, Middlesex. The overbridge station building uses anglicised Auhagen parts.

The LT steam shed is from an unknown kit whilst the water tower and depot are modified resin items. Meanwhile, the signal box and small depot hut are from the Severn Models range.

With Rossiter Rise complete and continuing its exhibition tour, Terry's my attention is turning to the next project – and something very different: an ex-Great North of Scotland Railway branch set in autumn. ■

READ MORE

Visit www.keymodelworld.com

Metropolitan 'F' class L.52 shunts a scratch-built sump wagon in the LT depot while a 1957 BR Eastleigh EMU enters the station and a North British Type 1 (later Class 16) rumbles through with a parcels train.

One of LT's new battery locomotives is posed outside the workshop alongside elderly 1901-built 0-6-2T L.52...

... while 'Ballast Driver' L.64 and another battery 'Slug' L.59 receive attention inside.

Lakeside

It's been a steep learning curve, but **GRAHAM FOULSTON** has finally settled on a layout that satisfies his eagerness to run a vibrant layout with various bells-and-whistles.

Right: **Nee-naw, nee-naw... The police have stopped a BMW in the high street in their fully illuminated Jaguar F Pace.**

Below: **An East Midlands Trains Class 158 eases into the front loop as a Class 66 and 68 pass on the centre roads with freight traffic. Many of the buildings and structures have been recycled from the original version of Lakeside.**

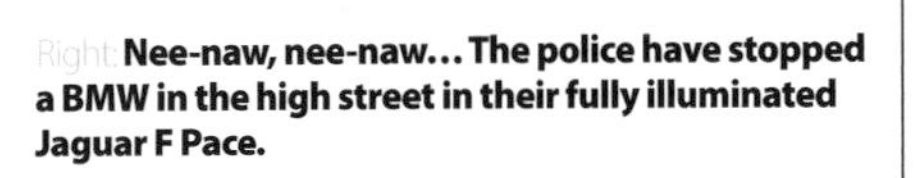

IF GRAHAM Foulston's experience is anything to go by, it's never too late to enter, or come back to, the wonderful world of railway modelling.

"Retirement was only a year or two away and I wanted to have a hobby that I could enjoy," he reflects. "I previously had hobbies like radio control model aircraft for several years, building several kit cars plus a varied number of other interests and wanted something different, something which would keep my mind occupied but it also had to be creative too."

A graphic designer and technical illustrator by trade for most of his career, and with a five-year mechanical engineering technician apprenticeship behind him, Graham "wanted something that would include all those things" and "it had to be creative, technical but most important of all, give me fun in the process".

So what better than a model railway?

The flame was ignited by an advert for Hornby's 'Brighton Belle' which he "fell in love with", rekindling childhood memories of seeing the real thing race through Three Bridges in West Sussex: "I just had to get it!"

Trials runs on the kitchen floor and a quick decision to equip it for DCC control left Graham "bitten by the bug".

"I already had a couple of old locomotives, some from my childhood and a few which I had bought over the years – just because I liked them – but at that time, no layout to run them on. I did a lot of research, mainly looking at YouTube videos on baseboard building, especially looking at other people just starting out in the hobby to give me some idea of what to do, what not to do, and what to expect. Things had changed so much since I last had a layout many years ago, it felt like I had to start from scratch again."

A reason for being

Before long, a series of baseboards had been erected to create a 16ft x 10ft layout structure in a spare room. Despite falling in love with the Thirties glamour of the 'Brighton Belle', the broad epoch for what would become Lakeside would be generic modern image – more of which anon. »

An intermodal freight rumbles through the centre roads behind DRS Class 68 68005 *Defiant*.

The manor house, salvaged from the original Lakeside layout, takes centre stage.

The YouTube modelling community pitched in with "help and support that I so needed at that time and still do even today" in response to Graham's own uploads recording progress on Lakeside.

To complement the "simple two track system", the hobby's new entrant "wanted a reason why every building, hill or bridge was there and not just put there because it seemed a good idea at the time".

"That was when I had the idea of building a manor house, which would be the central point… made up from seven different Metcalfe card kits of various buildings, sitting in its own substantial gardens and has a family all of its own living there who are major players within the Lakeside story."

However, after five years building, Graham found that he had become dissatisfied with his efforts.

"The layout was quite well advanced in its build state, but I was becoming more and more frustrated with it for various reasons, primarily because I had fallen into the trap that I was creating this layout from other peoples' suggestions: 'put a point here, put a double slip there'. It was hard work operating a complex track layout, plus I was finding out that my track laying was not what it should be. With a heavy heart I decided to take it all up and start afresh."

Lakeside v2 was born!

'Ooohs and aaahs'

Not only would the layout be refitted, but so would the room in which it resided, primarily by fitting air conditioning: "Gone would be the days of freezing cold winter days and sweltering hot summers in the 'train room'."

As well an improved working environment, this would help keep stock in good order and prevent baseboards warping.

Despite earlier frustrations, a lot of the scenics and buildings were rescued from Lakeside v1 so that its replacement would retain a similar feel.

However, a change of focus saw the new Lakeside develop with less emphasis on busy trackwork, instead focusing on scenic "points of interest".

"I wanted some parts of the new layout to be interactive so if friends came round then they could get involved and enjoy the fun of operating some of the scenes as well as run trains," Graham reveals.

Three months' work alone resulted in the creation of an operating passenger lift between Lakeside station platforms and Kingsway High Street level. "I'm proud of the way it works", he says. »

"With a heavy heart I decided to take it all up and start afresh."

GRAHAM FOULSTON

Lakeside is full of working features, including lighting, a Train-Tech destination display and an operational lift.

Kingsway Bus Station is built from a former Corgi kit and has been detailed inside with lighting and waiting passengers. The Duple Dominant II is a working vehicle which has been fitted with a Faller Car System mechanism.

The live action continues on the high street with the Faller road system of moving vehicles against the backdrop of lighted buildings.

Lakeside village, on the other side of the layout, features some personal touches. Two cyclists (one taking a dog along for the ride in a carrier) represent Graham, his wife and dog Ruby. There's also a replica of the thatched cottage that the couple call home.

"I think my favourite scene on the layout and one which has given me the most satisfaction," says Graham, "has to be the Magnorail cyclist moving around their track within the village area, creating many 'ooohs and aaahs' when people see it in action."

HST to 'Big Boy'

The stock featured on these pages reflects the general contemporary flavour of Lakeside, including Class 800, Network Rail New Measurement Train (HST), Class 70 hauled stone train, East Midlands Trains Class 158, Class 66 and DRS Class 68.

But, the whole rail scene era can be changed in under an hour.

Explains Graham: "My rolling stock, like many model railway enthusiast's, has grown considerably since I first started the layout and I have stock which I like rather than a certain era or region."

Therefore, rostered turns range from a Great Northern Railway 'Atlantic' through to a Union Pacific 'Big Boy': "just because I like them!"

Control is via Roco's Z2, which combines a Wifi network with an iPad to operate the layout, complete with inbuilt locomotive database with customised images. Fitting the layout's interactive nature, a number of locomotives are equipped with sound.

"They say a model railway is never finished and I can see now that it is very true," Graham

Non-stop action! Four trains – a Class 158, Network Rail Measurement Train, Class 70 hauled stone train and Class 800 – criss-cross on the transition curve between Lakeside town and village.

LAKESIDE TRACK DIAGRAM (Not to scale)

16ft

10ft

KEY				
1 Bus station	5 Station building	9 Multi-storey car park	13 Future scenic area	17 Public house
2 Bus stop	6 Platform buildings	10 To future extension	14 Future lake	18 Thatched cottage
3 Town buildings	7 Canopy	11 Steam sheds	15 Viaduct	19 Cottages
4 Platform	8 Faller return loop	12 Lifting section	16 Manor house and grounds	20 Cycle loop

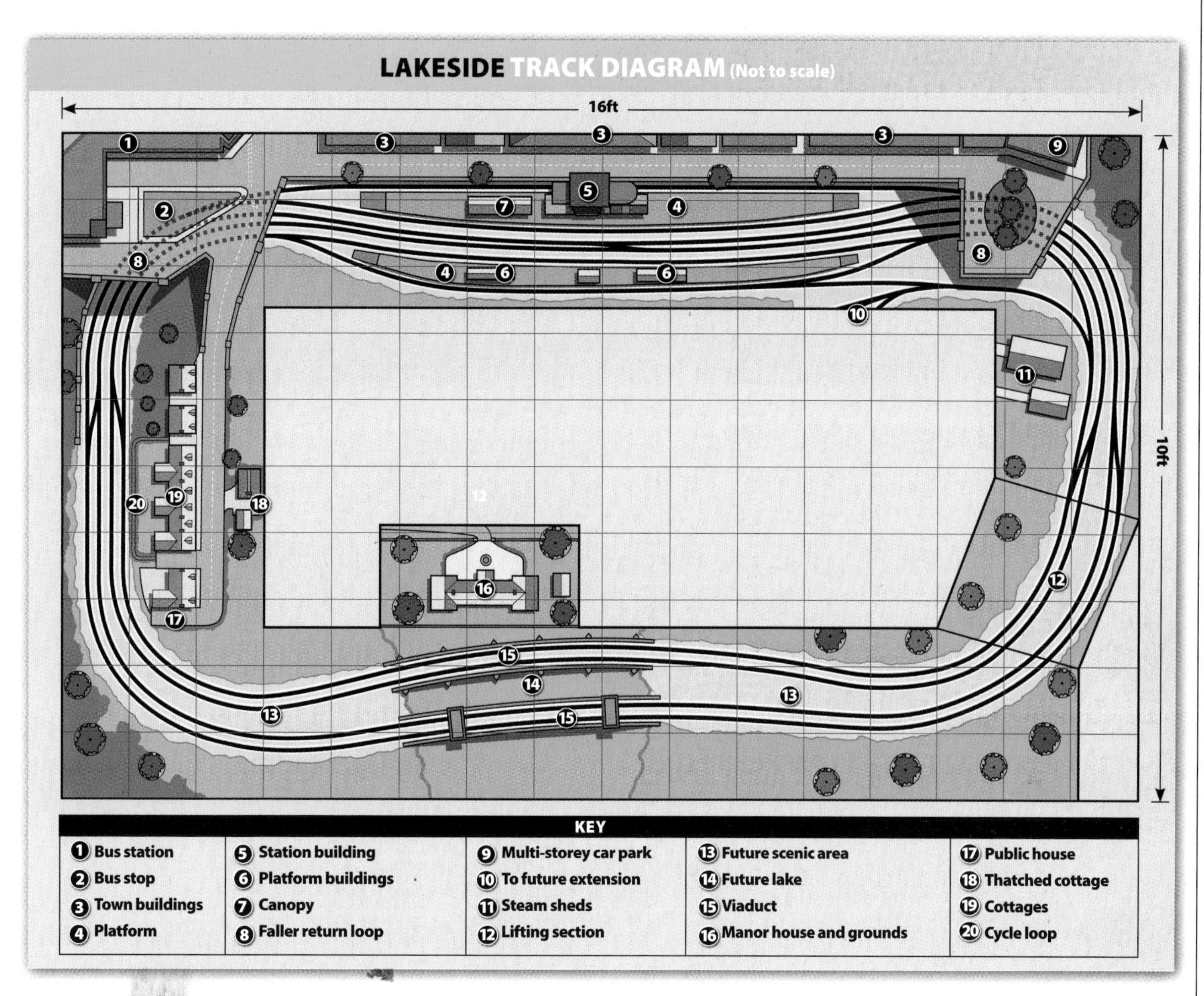

muses. "I'm sure that once I think Lakeside is completed, then I will look around and see that a certain area needs a slight 'tweak'.

"None of this would have been possible if it hadn't been for all the help and support I have had along the way, mainly from the good folk who follow me on YouTube and Facebook." ■

READ MORE

Visit www.keymodelworld.com

A new arrival on Lakeside is Heljan's 'OO' gauge model of unique EWS maroon and gold liveried Class 33 33030, alongside a bookstall, no doubt stocked with the latest issue of *Hornby Magazine*!

Halifax Powell *Street*

A main line terminus in a small bedroom! **PETE DURANT** proves the art of the possible with his evocative rendition of the West Riding area of Yorkshire in the 1960s.

PHOTOGRAPHY, PETE DURANT

IN PETE DURANT'S miniaturised world, 1890-era plans to bring the London & North Western Railway into Halifax Powell Street actually materialised, thus challenging the dominance of the Great Northern railway in this industrial revolution centric Yorkshire town.

The "element of reality" of his model railway is based around the premise that the LNWR wanted to impose itself in the West Riding area, and Halifax in particular, attracted by its famous wealth of woollen, carpet, machine tool and sugar confectionary industries.

In Pete's mind's eye, given the secondary main line terminus was a latecomer to the town, the LNWR ended up with a cramped site, built within a cutting and almost entirely surrounded by imposing retaining walls.

The excuse for being able to squeeze so much railway – a fully-fledged terminus and Motive Power Depot (MPD) – into a spare bedroom was therefore warranted.

A railway mill town scene now sadly vanished, but effectively encapsulated in model form by Pete Durant. A Sulzer Type 2 growls into Halifax Powell Street while a Derby three-car DMU eases away with a local service.

Halifax Powell Street ended up bound into joint ownership between the LMS and LNER.

A 1940s Luftwaffe air raid sadly spelt the end of the station canopy, which would have provided far superior protection than the stark post-war era bare platforms.

After nationalisation the station became part of the North Eastern Region of British Railways, before being transferred to the London Midland Region during the 1958 national boundary changes, the era depicted here.

Goods trains are dealt with off-scene and, once their brake vans have been shunt released by the station pilot, are required to pull into the short parcels platform before reversing along an 80-yard spur into the goods yards.

This "fictional justification" anchors this modest-size, yet impressively busy, layout in a believable situation, emphasised by the many impressive buildings that are faithful replicas of real examples from the Halifax area.

Imagination is a wonderful thing…

Peppercorn 'K1' 62059 passes beneath Bridge 61 while shunting a short rake of vans as freshly turned 'Dub Dee' 90707 rolls onto shed.

Dickensian mills

Moving into his first house in 2015 sealed Pete's "magical Venn diagram of spare time, space and income" to make his "first attempt at a 'proper' model railway after childhood trainsets".

Images of not only Halifax, but neighbouring Huddersfield and Bradford, plus "fantastic layouts" including the late Dave Shakespeare's Tetleys Mills and Manchester Model Railway Society's Dewsbury Midland sowed further seeds of inspiration for Pete's own 'OO' slice of Yorkshire.

"I wanted to replicate the imposing scale of the architecture and include Dickensian mills and sooty black terrace houses synonymous with the area," says Pete.

Hours poring over *LNWR Portrayed* by Jack Nelson had already sparked the motivation long before the house move. A pair of Wills northlight engine shed kits were 'bashed' in 2008, complete with scratch-built interior, to create a layout-ready, four-road MPD diorama.

After settling on a trackplan using deisgn software Scarm, it was time to make the baseboards. Because the3.5ft depth of the scenic section would ultimately be hard to reach across, this was made in two stages with the rearmost baseboards installed first.

These were covered in 3mm cork (for sound deadening). Peco 75 flatbottom track came next (with increased sleeper spacings); then ballasted (Carrs 2mm Dark Grey Ballast on the main lines and fine Ash Ballast for the carriage sidings and MPD); and wire-in-tube point control installed.

The radii for the 'point rodding' was kept as large as possible, but etched brass angled cranks were used for the points along the front edge of the layout. The wires were routed to one of two control panels (one for the scenic section, one for the fiddle yard) consisting of slide switches providing the mechanical actuation and changes in frog polarity.

Protecting the main line points are two modified bracket signals, displaying a 'starter' and 'shunt ahead' signal for each platform. These are modified using Ratio (477) LNWR square-posts as a basis, with Alan Gibson etch brass cranks (replacing the as-supplied

Every inch an urban setting... Fairburn 2-6-4T 42094 waits with its 'stopper' just as Bo-Bo D5017 arrives past the detailed Bachmann Scenecraft signal box.

"I wanted to replicate the imposing scale of the architecture and include Dickensian mills."

PETE DURANT

plastic ones), with linkages made from guitar string. The signals are controlled with a MegaPoints Servo Controller Unit driving cheap miniature servos via toggle switches.

DCC train control is provided by an NCE Power Cab.

The fiddle yard was formed of cassettes; "an absolute necessity for operational interest", whereas dead-end sidings would have been too restrictive.

Rolling stock is a mixture of mainly Bachmann and Hornby items, variously detailed, renumbered and weathered.

Building blend

The standard LNWR signal box is from Bachmann Scenecraft's extensive 'ready-to-plonk' range, with a detailed interior (Ratio) and finer external handrails fitted, with the accompanying resin coal stage/water tower given similar handrail treatment.

A South Eastern Finecast's turntable kit was beefed-up with spares from the old-faithful Dapol model, with the deck given a

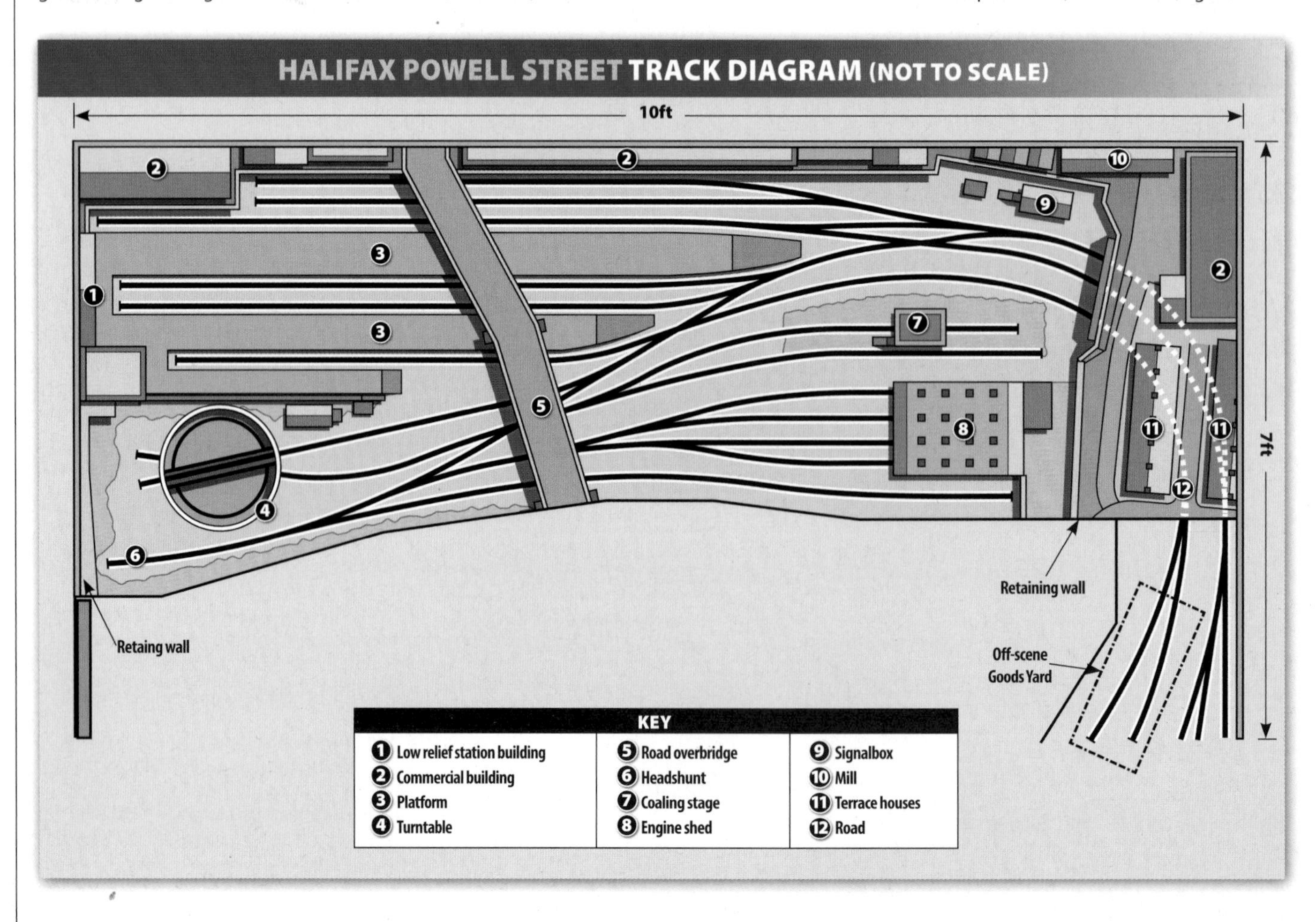

HALIFAX POWELL STREET TRACK DIAGRAM (NOT TO SCALE)

10ft

7ft

Retaing wall

Retaining wall

Off-scene Goods Yard

KEY		
1 Low relief station building	5 Road overbridge	9 Signalbox
2 Commercial building	6 Headshunt	10 Mill
3 Platform	7 Coaling stage	11 Terrace houses
4 Turntable	8 Engine shed	12 Road

The first light of day begins to penetrate the sky as a commuter service shares station space with parcels and goods traffic.

typical wooden plank finish using balsa wood and Wills chequer plate between the rails.

All of the other, tightly-packed structures are handmade using 1.5mm mounting card shells covered in a variety of different grades of Slaters Plastikard products: 7mm Dressed Stone and 7mm Cotswold Stone for the retaining walls; 7mm Brick and 4mm Course Grey Medium for the station, mills and commercial buildings; and 2mm Dressed Stone for the terrace houses. "Although these are not all 4mm scale items as sold, they seem to fit the size and variety that can be seen in the area," Pete explains.

The buildings were sprayed with a base colour of Humbrol acrylic Desert Tan before dry brushing several coats of assorted browns and a little black to highlight the relief and dull and dirty the finish.

Gutters were made from Plastruct half round styrene and downpipes were from waste solid core copper wire with soldered brackets. Roof tiles are from 100gsm paper, painted with Payne's grey acrylic and dusted with talcum powder.

For the windows, glass microscope slides were glued onto the inside wall before individual pieces of 0.5mm and 0.8mm square section styrene were cut and glued in place with plastic weld solvent to form the frames.

The results speak for themselves.

Riding no more

With both daytime and night-time modes, plus a surfeit of train movement permutations, Pete describes the final result as "an enjoyable layout to operate with a variety of moves and sequences to keep me entertained".

Despite that, Halifax Powell Street was recently dismantled to enable a new, larger layout to be built. The accompanying images provide a lasting legacy of a short-lived West Riding classic.

We can't wait to see what comes next... ■

READ MORE

Visit www.keymodelworld.com

Below: **A splendid rug dries in the backyard of a typical row of West Riding terraces, overshadowed by Halifax's 'Satanic Mills'.**

Essence of *Swindon*

Want to show off big main line locomotives, but haven't space for long trains? **MARK WILSON'S** magnificent cameo of Swindon Works shows just what you can achieve, with help from mirrors.

PHOTOGRAPHY, RICHARD WATSON

REGION	SCALE	GAUGE	SIZE	PERIOD	CONTROL
WESTERN	4mm:1ft	'OO', 16.5mm	5ft x 2ft	1961-1986	DC/DCC SWITCHABLE

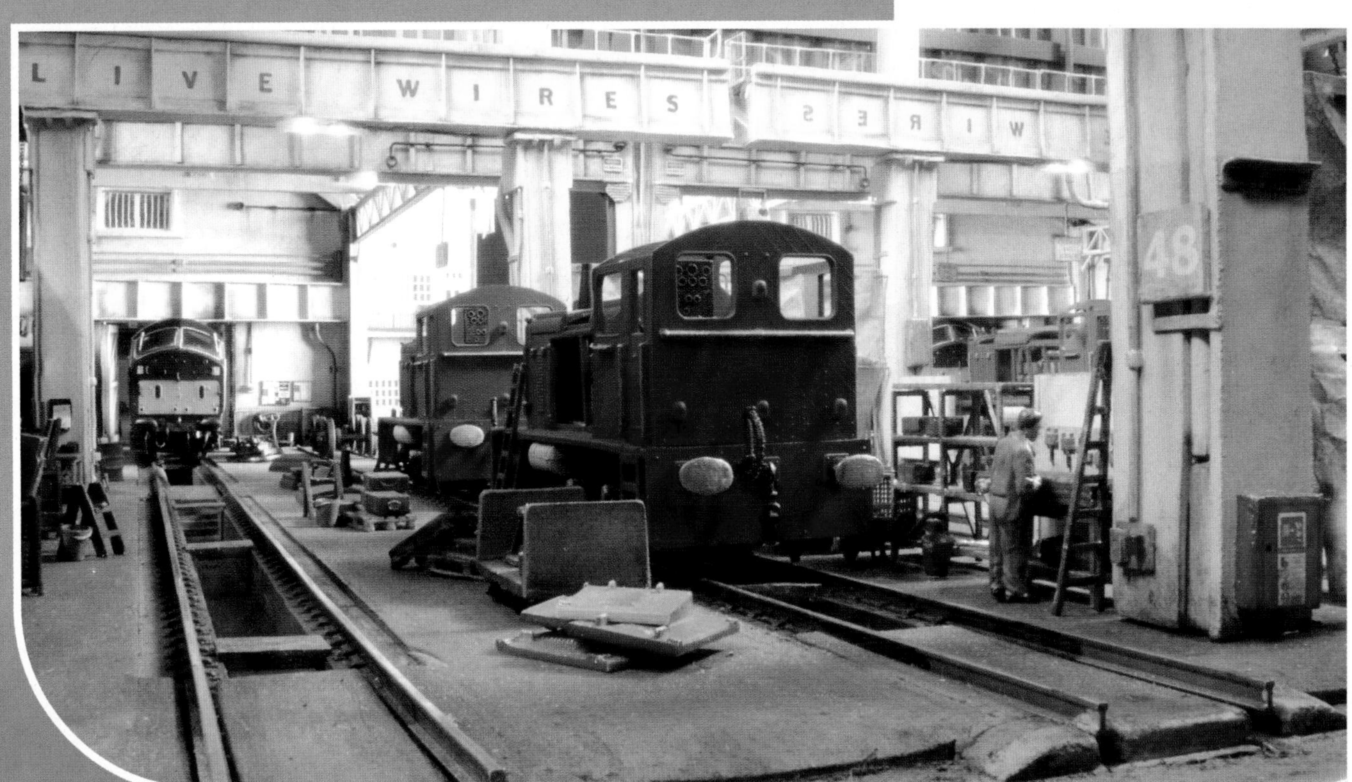

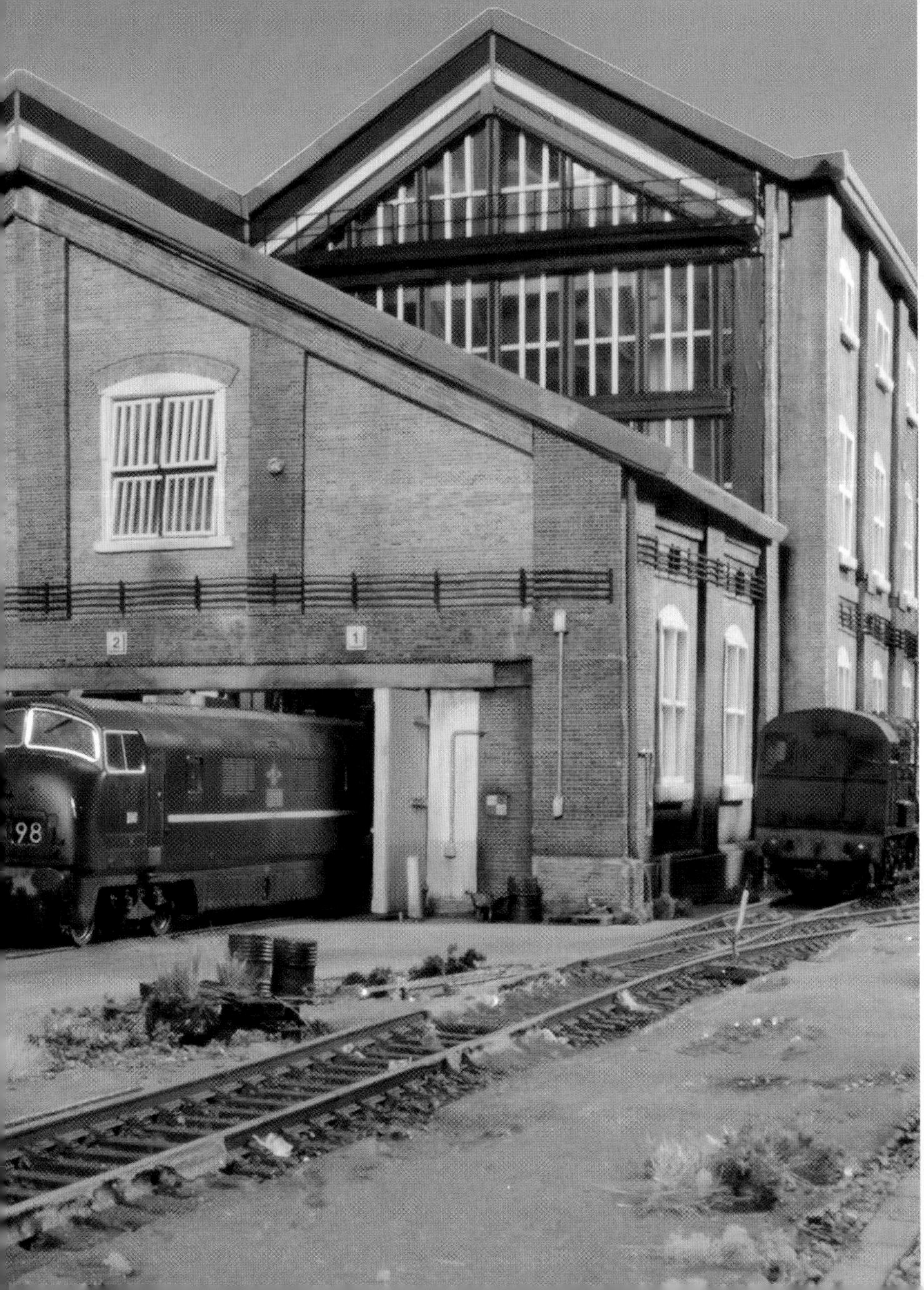

"TO BE honest it's not a very interesting track plan", Mark Wilson admits. He even calls himself a "modelling cheat".

Few would agree with such a modest assessment, even just by clapping eyes on these scenes of his homage to the once great Swindon Works is likely to elicit a response of worthy admiration.

Most would instead agree that his ambition to "build an instantly recognisable model" of 'A Shop' was wholly successful. At first glance, you'd be fooled into thinking that Mark's Essence of Swindon was a room-filler; rather, the scenic section is a smidge over 5ft. Smaller than the average domestic desk.

Mark again confesses that he "hangs his head in shame" that he never visited Swindon Works before closure in 1986, even though by that stage he had become "hooked" on hydraulics, in particular the Westerns, Hymeks and Warships.

His diorama-cum-layout therefore seeks to redress what he missed.

Even so, Mark was able to see the site close-up in the mid-1990s after what buildings remained had opened as a retail outlet centre, with extensive housing developments yet to finally obliterate all trace of the hallowed 'A Shop' where the Great Western Railway's most famous locomotives were manufactured.

Having wondered round the Wiltshire shopping centre, Mark pondered whether in model form it was possible to "bring it back to a standard where enthusiasts would recognise it at a glance?"

Such a diorama would be "ideal" without the space to run full length trains of up to 12 carriages. »

Left: **Even as a representative slice of the towering mass 'A Shop' is unmistakable. A 'Hymek' and 'Warship' flank the unique shape of 1949-built Gas Turbine No. 18000.**

Top: **A pair of '04' shunters undergo heavy overhaul. These are modified plastic Dapol kits.**

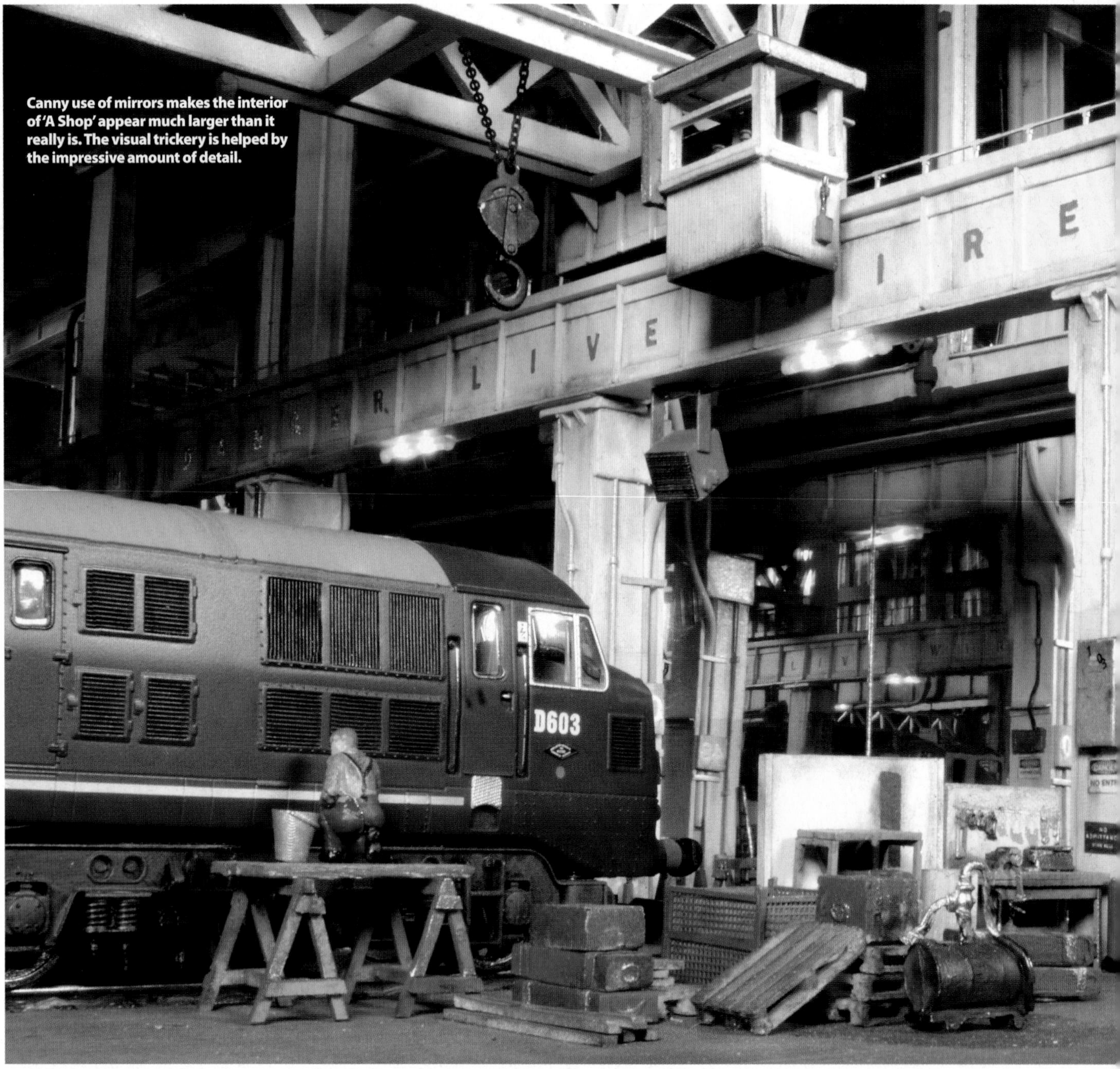

Canny use of mirrors makes the interior of 'A Shop' appear much larger than it really is. The visual trickery is helped by the impressive amount of detail.

SWINDON WORKS **TRACK DIAGRAM** (NOT TO SCALE)

KEY

1 To/from off-scene storage yard	3 Staircase to subway	5 Removable fuel tanks	7 Great Western Main Line	9 Backscene
2 Weigh House	4 AE Shop	6 Storage line	8 Removable roof	10 To London

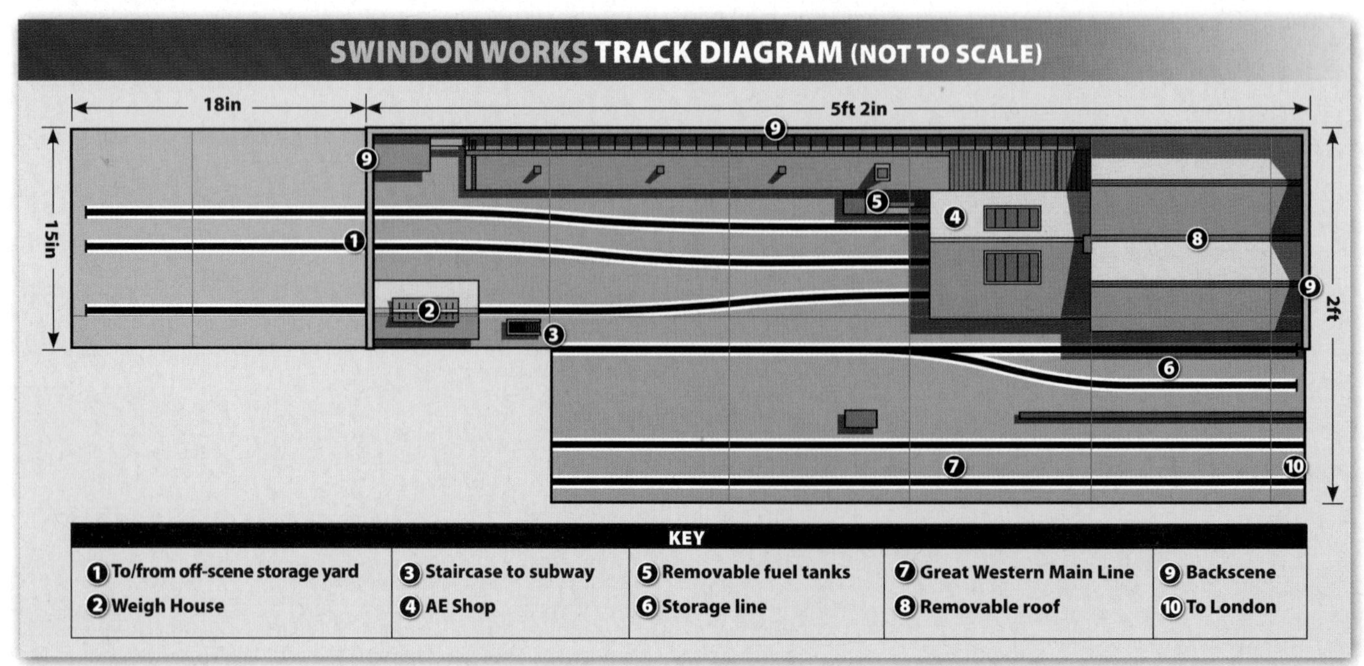

The compact nature of Essence of Swindon makes it just as suited to being used layout as being displayed as a diorama.

That inspired an "internet shopping spree of books and photographs" in pursuit of gleaning as much detail about the works as possible. Membership of the *Swindon Works – End of the Line* group on Facebook elicited more material.

"When I finally plucked up the courage to ask a question, I not only had answers, but unpublished photos with detail that only the men that worked on the site would know," Mark recounts. "Not only did I get my answers, it then sparked extremely and fascinating conversations between ex-employees."

That was just as well, because without this vital information because Mark readily accepts that he is "actually not that good at making things up when modelling buildings and landscapes… as I have to copy reality and only then they seem to turn out slightly convincing".

> *"The stories and recollections of the works that have turned this model into a time machine."*
>
> **MARK WILSON**

Smoke and mirrors

The plan was to keep it small with just the exterior face of the 'AE' building so the locomotives could sit just outside the doors.

Indeed, so far as track plans go, this is "not a very interesting one", consisting of seven parallel lines and just one turnout – and there wasn't space for the traverser. But what Essence of Swindon lacks in operational scope is more than made up by its theatrical ambience and attention to detail.

Then Mark thought, "well if I take this to exhibitions then I will need the locomotives »

The removable roof reveals a spectacular display of trusses and the mobile crane.

Left: **The Gas Turbine goes through final checks in the Weigh House.**

Opposite: **The adaptable nature of the model means that the steam era can also be represented. A Large Prairie await works attention… or perhaps a date with the scrapman.**

Below: **A 'Western' is suspended in mid-air alongside a stripped-down 'Warship'.**

to appear emerging from the exit doors… without them being seen".

"I then studied what was behind the doors and my interest grew and grew. Over Christmas 2020 I set about modelling one of the wonderful 100-ton cranes powered by two Ransoms & Rapier of Ipswich motors. Yes, that's how I spent Christmas Day, at the modelling table, but with 'Lockdown 2' in place I had nowhere to go anyway, so why not?"

The ambition was to give the impression of the "vast Cathedral style expanse" that 'A Shop' was famous for, but in a "very small space".

"I had two options: to call my local 'Time Lord' and borrow his Tardis, or use mirrors to the rear and righthand side," Mark quips.

The mirrors are 3mm thick plastic, which enabled them to be readily cut to shape and are simple, yet highly effective way of amplifying the sense of space. "I call myself a modelling cheat", he surmises.

"All the buildings have removable section sides, roofs and rear viewing panels so I can take photographs inside the buildings from many different angles," Mark explains.

The buildings are made from card covered in Scalescenes brick and slate papers. The main building windows were not readily available to the size required so I had to make these from scratch counting the bricks to work out the rough size.

Time machine

A novel feature is that the scene's epoch can be chopped and changed by swapping details around, not just locomotives.

In the 25-year steam and diesel changeover period that the layout can depict, two large fuel tanks appeared as chimneys disappeared, and the timber doors were replaced with roller shutters; all of which are interchangeable.

Such was the organised chaos of Swindon that Mark says how "surprising it was to look at archive images only look again days later and spot the items I'd missed".

"From buckets, paint tins, tools, benches, cupboards, pallets, oil drums, trollies, fire extinguishers, cables, pipes, electrical distribution boards, waste bins, tool chests, notice boards, the list is endless," he says.

Many of these were either bought as 3D-printed items or MDF laser kits.

The works scene was completed on the lefthand side with the representation of the Weigh House, where locomotives would be balanced following attention in the main works.

"More information came flooding in, allowing me to re-create what once was, the six weighing machines made by Henry Pooley & Sons 1930."

Mark adds: "It's all the stories and recollections of the works that have turned this model into a time machine", even if one ex-employee remarked "that the floor on my model is far too clean!" ■

READ MORE

Visit www.keymodelworld.com

Shenston Road

Blue, green and everything in between… **GREG BROOKES** reveals his diesel centric, urban masterpiece that has taken more than 20 years to create.

PHOTOGRAPHY, MIKE WILD

'Hymek' D7001, repainted blue from green in March 1971, hauls a string of empty hopper wagons betwixt the houses of Shenston Road and Metchells & Butlers brewery.

A clean but slightly shabby Class 46 D163 *Leicestershire and Derbyshire Yeomanry* (also known as 'The Lady') betrays evidence of a replacement cab door.

SHENSTON ROAD captures the post-steam period in all its shabby glory, when locomotives were often in poor external condition and others were fresh and gleaming in the new colour schemes. This late 1960s-early 1970s changeover period blended the BR greens and maroons of an earlier age with the striking new blue and grey of the corporate image era.

Greg Brookes set out on his project of a lifetime in a 27ft x 8ft 6in, purpose-built railway 'den'. This has enabled him to create a layout chock-full of gradients, a hidden storage yard, a large through station, a steelworks (complete with exchange sidings), industrial buildings and street scenes spread across 360 degrees of scenery.

The station owes its origins to the former Great Western Railway route between Birmingham and Wolverhampton where Greg grew up, although its layout takes inspiration from Hereford. On the opposite side of the room, the steelworks has shades of Llanwern, Port Talbot and Panteg.

Simply put, "I wanted to see full length trains running in an urban and industrial setting", Greg reflects.

Planning of the layout took three months. And no wonder given its complexity; a figure of eight with the station on the upper level on one side. The mainline curves round to the other side, down a gradient in front of the steelworks before disappearing underground to reach the storage yard (which can be accessed by lifting the hinged scenic station section above). From there, the double track mainline climbs back out the other end, swinging round and underneath the steelworks on its own shelf before emerging just above where it exited the scene at the other end.

Its complexity and construction style mean that Shenston Road is a permanent fixture in its railway room and will never go out to exhibitions.

Throw in the protracted nature of handbuilt track, it's no surprise that it took eight years to reach the first landmark of fully functioning layout, although Greg acknowledges that "through shift work and family commitments it did begin to stall at one time".

"Fortunately," he continues, "Kier Hardy of Wibdenshaw and Hornsey Broadway fame moved into the area and we became firm friends. His help and enthusiasm reinvigorated the project."

BRUTE force

The result of their effort, with similarly appreciated input from Bill Connelly, Martin Crowe and Paul James, is seriously impressive.

The station is scratchbuilt (apart from the GWR footbridge, which started life as a Hornby kit). The platforms are extensively detailed with all the features of the period including BRUTE trolleys, conventional trolleys (with trainspotters resting on them, as well as luggage and mail sacks), staff, lamps and more.

The backdrop of industrial buildings are a combination of scratchbuilt and modified European outline kits.

Terraced houses are detailed front and back, and, if you look closely along the railway »

Left: **A 'Janus' 0-6-0 shunts specialist molten steel wagons outside the billet caster building.**

Below: **Split headcode English Electric 'Type 4' D337 restarts its mixed freight from the centre tracks at Shenston Road. GWR lower quadrant signals set the scene for this Western Region location.**

You could imagine this is 'N' gauge, such is the magnitude of Greg Brooke's model. A coal train wends its way from the storage sidings beneath the steelworks toward Shenston Road station behind 'Peak' D4.

cutting sides you will rubbish tipped down the banks from the alleyways.

On steelworks' side, the topography is multi-level. A single track branch rises up from the station on the opposite side of the layout to reach the exchange sidings.

The far end of the (kit and scratchbuilt) steelworks focuses on the internal railway systems for which a number of specialist wagons have been made to operate with a fleet of industrial shunters. These include the Golden Valley Hobbies Yorkshire Engine Co 'Janus' 0-6-0. Their dedicated depot is accessed via a bridge back over the mainline.

Everything that you see inside the railway fence line derives inspiration from Greg's first-hand experience as a driver.

"Before the internet the industrial scene was the most difficult to research as photographs weren't as freely available as they are now. Luckily my job took me to Shotton, Llanwern, Port Talbot and Cardiff GKN at Tidal Sidings where I managed to get plenty of pictures of the steelworks industry during my breaks.

"Another unusual feature is the track which I have built in a distressed manner by widening the gauge subtly (but so trains will still run) as well as introducing lumps and bumps in the rails and at joints.

"This is where my career has helped – being in the cab I've been able to see first-hand how the railway really looks at track level and I've aimed to include as much of that as possible into the layout.

"Everything on the layout is weathered - whether it is a building, road vehicle, structure, locomotive or a piece of rolling stock. This is really important to me as I want the whole scene to blend together so that no single item stands out too much against the crowd."

Train control

Analogue control is used throughout using a trio of controllers to operate different sections; two for the Up and Down mainlines and a third for the steelworks branch and sidings.

"Usually, I only have one train running on each mainline circuit," Greg says, "although with maximum concentration it is possible to have two following each other. However, with analogue control I have to keep a close eye on their performance so that the two trains don't catch each other up.

"Another enjoyable aspect of the operational side is bringing a train into the »

Birmingham City Transport Atlantean and Fleetline double-decker buses watch over Shenston Road's busy junction and yard as 'Type 3' 6972 growls past. The single line branch to the steelworks passes beneath the arched bridge at the far end.

> *"I want the whole scene to blend together so that no single item stands out too much against the crowd"*
>
> **GREG BROOKES**

BRUTE trollies... a vivid memory for anyone who stood on stations in the 1970s.

1971's *Get Carter* and the 1968 Ford Capri, immortalised in 4mm:1ft scale.

Above: **White goods, a mattress and toilet seat are among some of the dumped lineside debris.**

loops, either in front of the steelworks or at the station and allowing it to be overtaken by a following service. This recreates another caveat of the real railway which is still a daily occurrence."

Point control is a mixture of electric and mechanical depending on how easily accessible each is.

The locomotive fleet meanwhile is representative of the final years of the 1960s and the early 1970s prior to the introduction of the TOPS numbering system. Running this period allows me to run the last of the Western Region diesel-hydraulics ("which are amongst my favouirtes" Greg adds) alongside diesel-electric traction coming from the Midland and Eastern regions.

Most of the locomotives are modified, detailed and renumbered ready-to-run products from Bachmann, Dapol, Heljan and Hornby.

All have been regauged to 'EM' gauge.

The fleet consists of classes 08, 14, 20, 22, 25, 31, 35, 37, 40, 42, 43, 44, 45, 46, 47 and 52. The rolling stock fleet is even more diverse and consists of ready-to-run, kit built, modified and scratchbuilt vehicles. Highlights include block rakes of Accurascale Cemflo cement tankers and HUO hoppers, the Murgatroyds chlorine tanks and Leather sulphuric acid tanks (both scratchbuilt), Gulf heavy oil 100ton TEA tankers and a huge number of steel wagons to suit traffic to and from the exchange sidings.

Even after 21 years, there are still continual additions to stock, as well as other areas being developed.

"This keeps the layout fresh and exciting," says Greg. "It will always have scope for being upgraded, modified and further detailed to improve upon what I have already built.

"I have gained great satisfaction from showing it to others, learning from fellow modellers and taking on their constructive feedback to continually upgrade it over the years. Building the layout has been a fantastic journey." ■

"I wanted to see full length trains running in an urban and industrial setting."

READ MORE

Visit www.keymodelworld.com

Right: **The mainlines travel down a gradient in front of the steelworks to reach the low level storage yard. A Brush Type 4 enters the loop while a pair of English Electric Type 1s tick over with a rake of HUO coal hoppers.**

SHENSTON ROAD TRACK DIAGRAM (Not to scale)

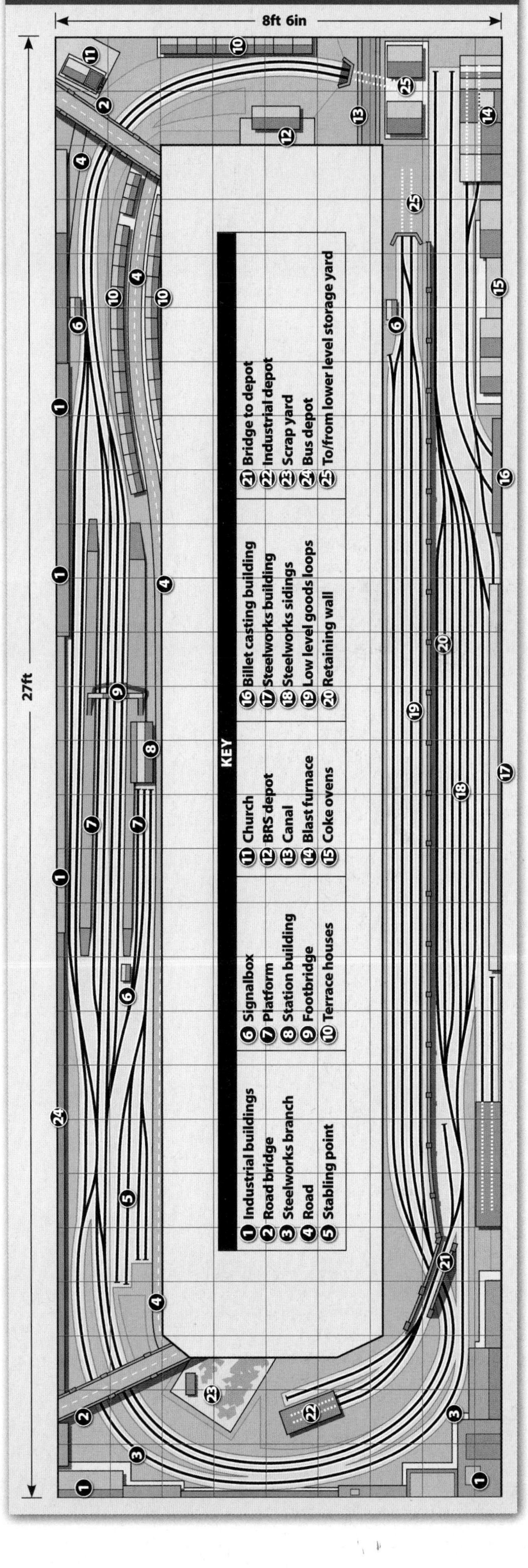

8ft 6in

27ft

KEY

1. Industrial buildings
2. Road bridge
3. Steelworks branch
4. Road
5. Stabling point
6. Signalbox
7. Platform
8. Station building
9. Footbridge
10. Terrace houses
11. Church
12. BRS depot
13. Canal
14. Blast furnace
15. Coke ovens
16. Billet casting building
17. Steelworks building
18. Steelworks sidings
19. Low level goods loops
20. Retaining wall
21. Bridge to depot
22. Industrial depot
23. Scrap yard
24. Bus depot
25. To/from lower level storage yard

Middleton-in-Teesdale

It's a bucolic slice of the 1930s North East reimagined in the Home Counties. The De Havilland Model Railway Society's **MIKE WORSLEY** tells the story of this old stager.

SOME RAILWAY locations simply cry out to be scaled down into model form. The North Eastern Railway's (NER) Middleton-in-Teesdale is a perfect example.

Opened in 1868, the terminus of the 7½ mile long Middleton-in-Teesdale branch terminated on the North Yorkshire side of the Tees, although the village it served was actually on the opposite side of the river in County Durham.

The station earned its particular operational quirk thanks to the nearby Ord & Maddison stone quarries, which had which had their own private exchange sidings to the left of the approaching main line. Loaded wagons would arrive from the quarries worked by one of its privately owned 'Y7' 0-4-0T engines for onward transport by NER, later the London and North Eastern Railway (LNER).

Another private siding led into the wood yard and sawmill.

The station had a single platform with a run-round loop as well as a single road shed, a couple of water tanks and a 45ft turntable. The shed and turntable were built a year after the opening of the branch. On the opposite side of the main line were the goods platform, cattle dock, coal drops and goods shed. The goods yard was served by a daily pick-up goods train from Barnard Castle.

The fascinating blend of infrastructure, brought to life by goods wagons being exchanged between the LNER and industrial branches, plus a healthy flow of 'ordinary' goods and passenger trains has made the De Havilland Model Railway Society's (DHMRS) Middleton-in-Teesdale an exhibition favourite for the best part of half a century. »

Loyal Worsdell 'J21' 0-6-0 1512 departs for Barnard Castle with a loaded train of crushed road stone. While that's happening, 'G5' 0-4-4T 2083 shunts the goods yard as an LNER 'Y3' 4wVBT takes charge of the stone quarry trains.

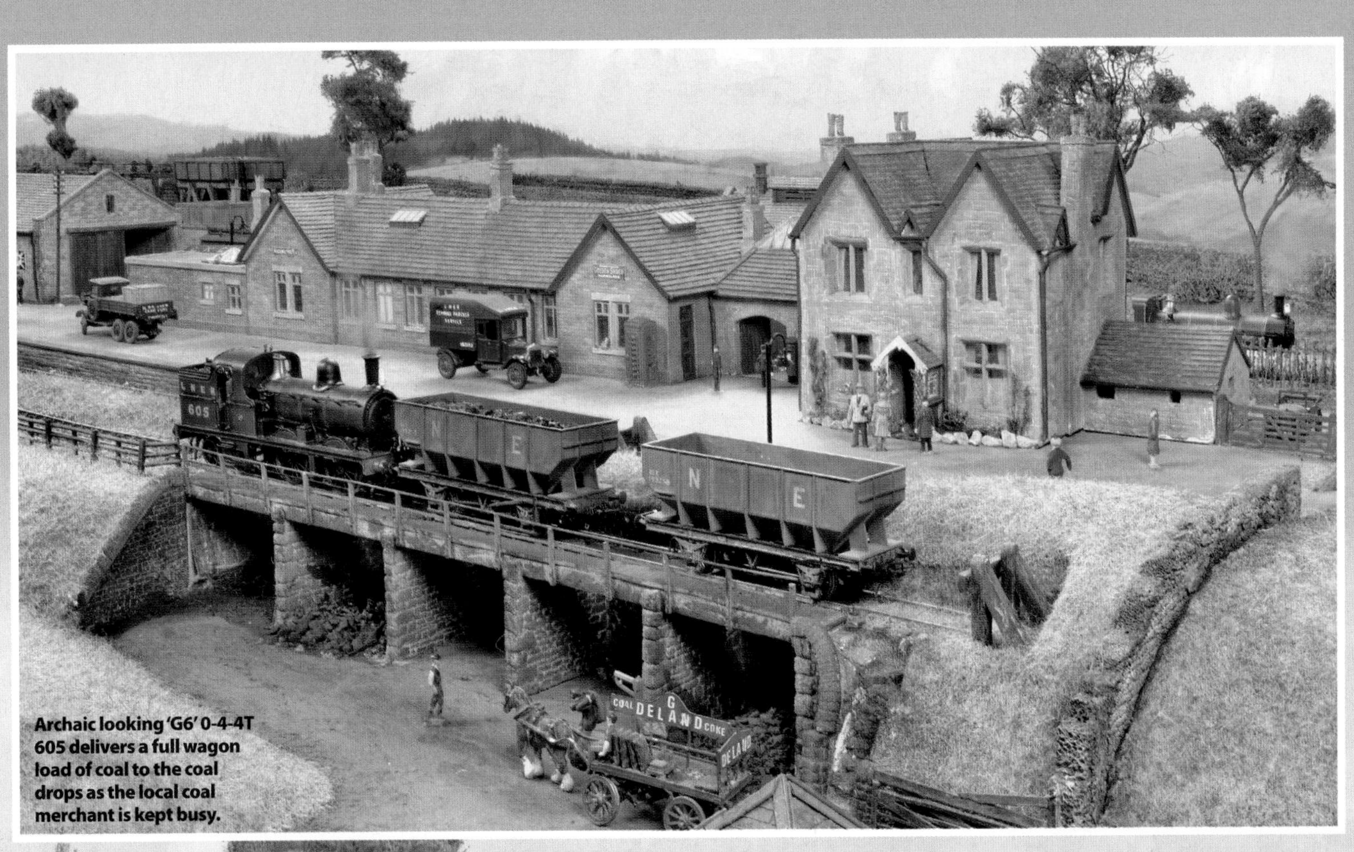

Archaic looking 'G6' 0-4-4T 605 delivers a full wagon load of coal to the coal drops as the local coal merchant is kept busy.

Havil layout, will travel

The layout started life in the 1970s as an add-on to the club's massive LMS layout, Havil Junction. With still room for an extension, it was decided to construct a branch line justifying Havil's junction status and so the NER-leaning contingent of the DHMRS successfully persuaded the other members that it should follow their favoured prototype, incorporating Middleton-in-Teesdale *and* Prospect Hill on the Whitby line.

"The project was to be detachable as an independent and portable exhibition layout," recounts member Mike Worsley. "This took many years to build, but when complete the layout was deemed too heavy to transport."

Things became even more problematic when after a couple of enforced moves, the club's latest home was much smaller, which meant Havil needed reducing in size and there was no room for Middleton as part of it.

The scenic area of Middleton is 17ft long and 3ft 3in wide. The depth presents a wide space to model the full railway operation at the station, overseen by operators Nigel Slatford and Phil Bicknell.

Explains Mike: "After many discussions between club members it was decided to scrap the old layout and build a much lighter and portable version of Middleton-in-Teesdale station."

Using lighter materials and supported on collapsible trestles, trolleys were built by members Steve Hughes and Colin Bloom to accommodate two baseboards each, designed to navigate the narrow doors and corridors when put into storage when not in use.

Insulating foam was selected for the new scenery contours because although rather messy it was quite easy to work with and static grass used for the first time – a scenic medium not available to the layout's original builders.

> *"It's an operator's layout rather than an exact scale model."*
>
> **MIKE WORSLEY**

Trees were made by various members of the club using their own methods and the stone walls were made from scribed insulating board.

"Before we removed the track from the original layout, plain wallpaper was laid onto the track to make indentations of the track plan," Mike continues. "This was then transferred onto the new boards. As the new baseboards were narrower than the originals, the track layout had to be slightly simplified to suit."

Peco Code 75 bullhead plain track has been mixed with Marcway points to suit various situations, with the prototype's ash ballast replicated.

The scratch-built turntable was salvaged from the original layout, the mechanism coming from an old record player!

The original signals were mostly used and modified where necessary using MERG electronics to operate the servo control.

Three way split

All of the buildings on Middleton are from the original layout, built using drawings from Ken Hoole's book on North Eastern branch line termini. Others were sourced by one of the Hertfordshire-based society's veteran members.

Details such as the boiler room at the saw mill can be seen and the rotating water wheel can be seen, plus the sound of the saw being used.

You can also hear the whistle from the daily goods train informing the signalman of his

Purposeful 'A5' 4-6-2T 1760 is about to depart Middleton for Darlington as former Great Eastern Railway 'E4' 7461 has just been turned, ready to back on to the engine shed.

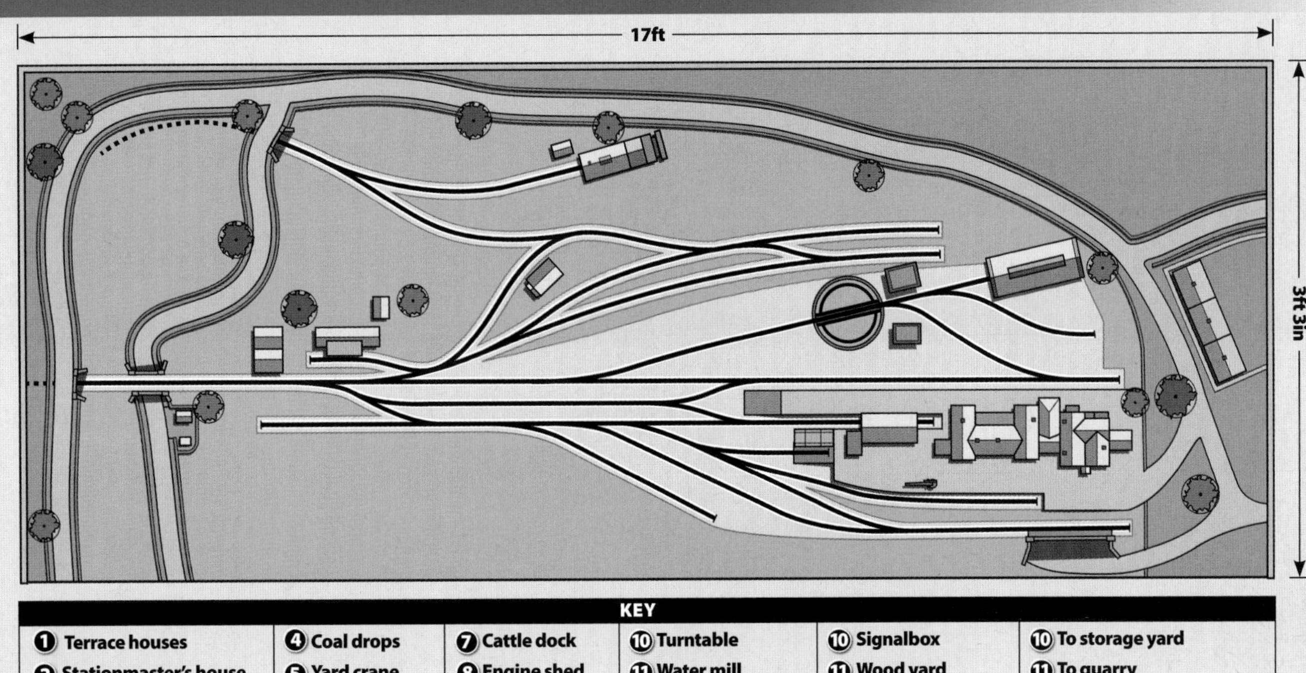

presence to enter the goods yard… and this is all without DCC.

"Operation is analogue because except for one member of the team digital control seemed alien to us more senior folk," Mike admits.

"We wanted a layout that would allow prototypical operation, with correct rolling stock and signalling of the period under LNER ownership from grouping until the start of the Second World War.," he continues. "In other words, it's an operator's layout rather than an exact scale model, also requiring enough movement to keep visitors occupied at exhibitions."

An operating sequence was devised keeping as near to the original timetable as possible but adding an extra couple of fictional passenger workings to add interest. The layout is run to a pre-arranged sequence, which takes approximately two hours to complete.

Three operators are split between operating the station (incoming trains, and engine shed movements); a second shunting both goods yards; and the third outgoing trains and storage yard.

The Ord & Maddison loaded stone wagons are propelled three at a time from the storage yard to the exchange sidings using the 'Y7' belonging to O&M or a 'Y3' on loan from the LNER. They are then taken forward via the main line back to the storage yard by either a 'J21' or 'J25' 0-6-0. For the empty wagons. the reverse sequence takes place.

Passenger trains arrive and the locomotive runs around via the turntable and water column.

Fry's delights

"Locomotives of the period were required for the layout and we were lucky enough to have master locomotive builder and collector Eric Fry - our most senior member - to solve this problem," says Mike. "He has built practically every class of engine that has run on the branch."

Eric is the editor and part author of the RCTS *Locomotives of the LNER* books, is still building model locomotives in his 90s. He has built most from London Road Models, Craftsman and Nucast kits.

Locomotives classes available service include: 'A5' 4-6-2T, 'A8' 4-6-2T, 'D3' 4-4-0, 'D17' 4-4-0, 'D23' 4-4-0, 'E4' 2-4-0, 'E5' 2-4-0, 'G5' 0-4-4T, 'G6' 0-4-4T, 'J21' 0-6-0, 'J25' 0-6-0, 'N9' 0-6-2T, Sentinel railcars, 'V1' 2-6-2T, 'Y3' 0-4-0T and 'Y7' 0-4-0T.

"The layout is more or less complete except little odd jobs such as trees, a couple of slightly damaged signals and the link," Mike adds.. "There is always something to do." ■

READ MORE

Visit www.keymodelworld.com

Sleepy branch line? Not a bit of it. An NER steam railcar approaches Middleton while a 'G5' and 'Y3' are captured propelling their respective wagons.

VISIT OUR ONLINE SHOP

TO VIEW OUR FULL RANGE OF SPECIAL MAGAZINES ABOUT **MODEL RAIL AND THE INDUSTRY**

KEY Shop

shop.keypublishing.com/specials

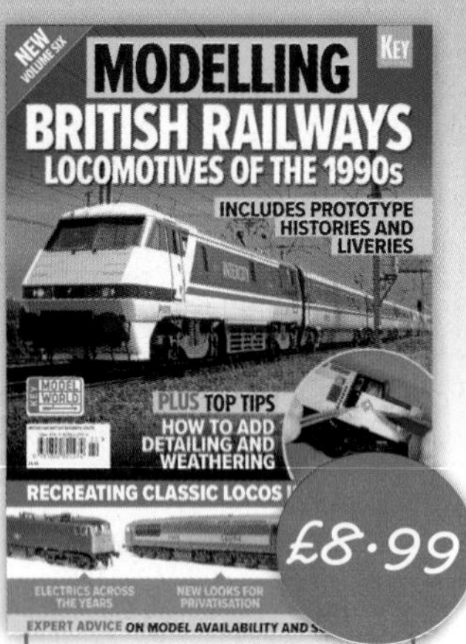

This eagerly awaited follow up to the popular Modelling British Railways series traces the development of the many diesel and electric classes through the decade as they transitioned from BR to private ownership.

In this highly anticipated follow up to his Greatest Layouts special published in 2022, Pete Waterman and the Railnuts group are taking on their biggest challenge yet.

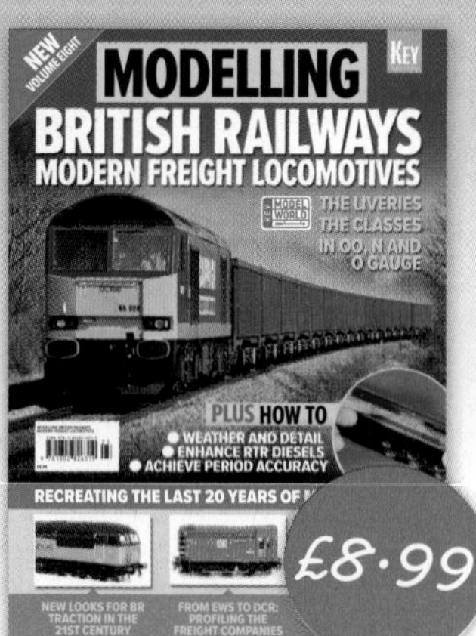

This new publication will show how to model a range of locomotives across two decades and in various scales while considering the numerous freight companies that have existed during this period.

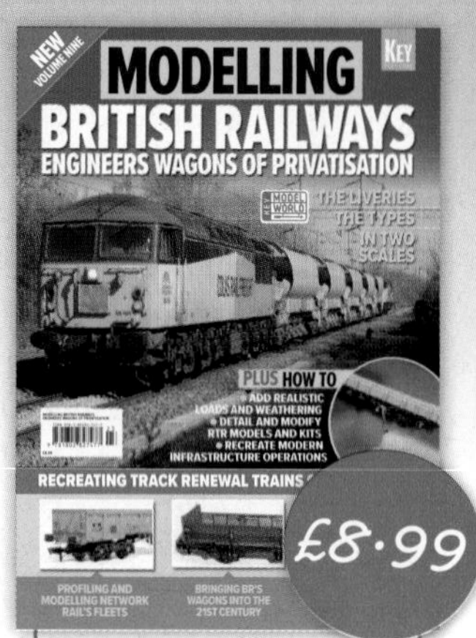

This publication will look at all the types used for ballast, sleeper and rail carrying over this period along with their operations and train formations.

The '90s arguably saw the greatest change of all in our rail system with privatisation, booming passenger numbers and the arrival of locomotives not built in the UK. This special publication traces those happenings in detail, year by year.

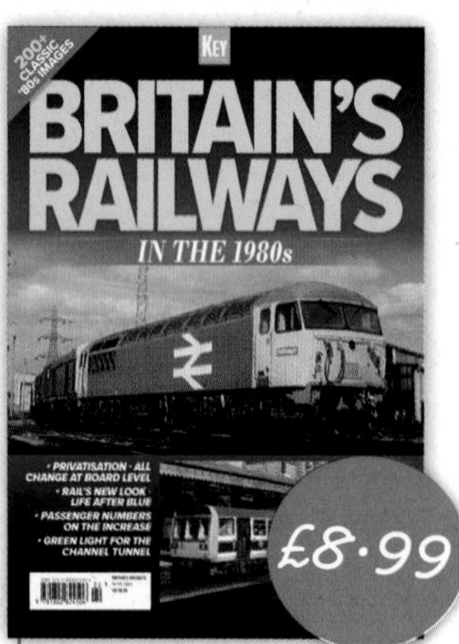

The 1980s was a decade of change for Britain's railways. All of these changes are charted year by year in this eagerly awaited fourth title in this lavishly illustrated series.

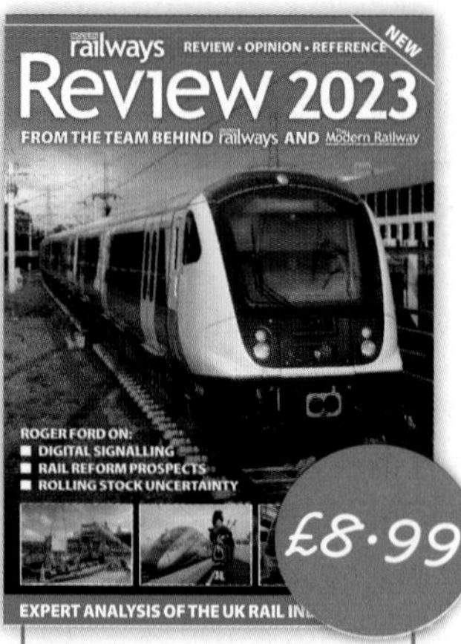

As well as reflecting of the successes of 2022, such as the opening of Crossrail and progress with HS2, the expert editorial team attempts to chart the likely way forward for the year to come.

Rail 123 is the only publication to list ALL vehicles in one easy to follow, colour coded list. The new edition of Rail 123 includes more than 20,000 changes and updates from the 2021-2022 edition.

FREE P&P* when you order online at...

shop.keypublishing.com/specials

SUBSCRIBERS don't forget to use your £2 OFF DISCOUNT CODE!

Call +44 (0)1780 480404 *(Monday to Friday 9am-5.30pm GMT)*

Also available from **W.H Smith** and all leading newsagents. Or download from **Pocketmags.com** or your native app store - search *Aviation Specials*

**Free 2nd class P&P on all UK & BFPO orders. Overseas charges apply.*

613/23

Penmouth and Curzon Street

Can't decide which of your favourite locations to model? Do them all at once! **MARK WILSON** reveals his London, Birmingham and South West inspired three-in-one layout.

PHOTOGRAPHY, MIKE WILD

A corrugated parcels bridge, BRUTE trolleys and a BR blue '47' is about as Seventies-Eighties as you can get. Brush-built 47402 *Gateshead* growls into Curzon Street with a cross country service from Penmouth in the West Country.

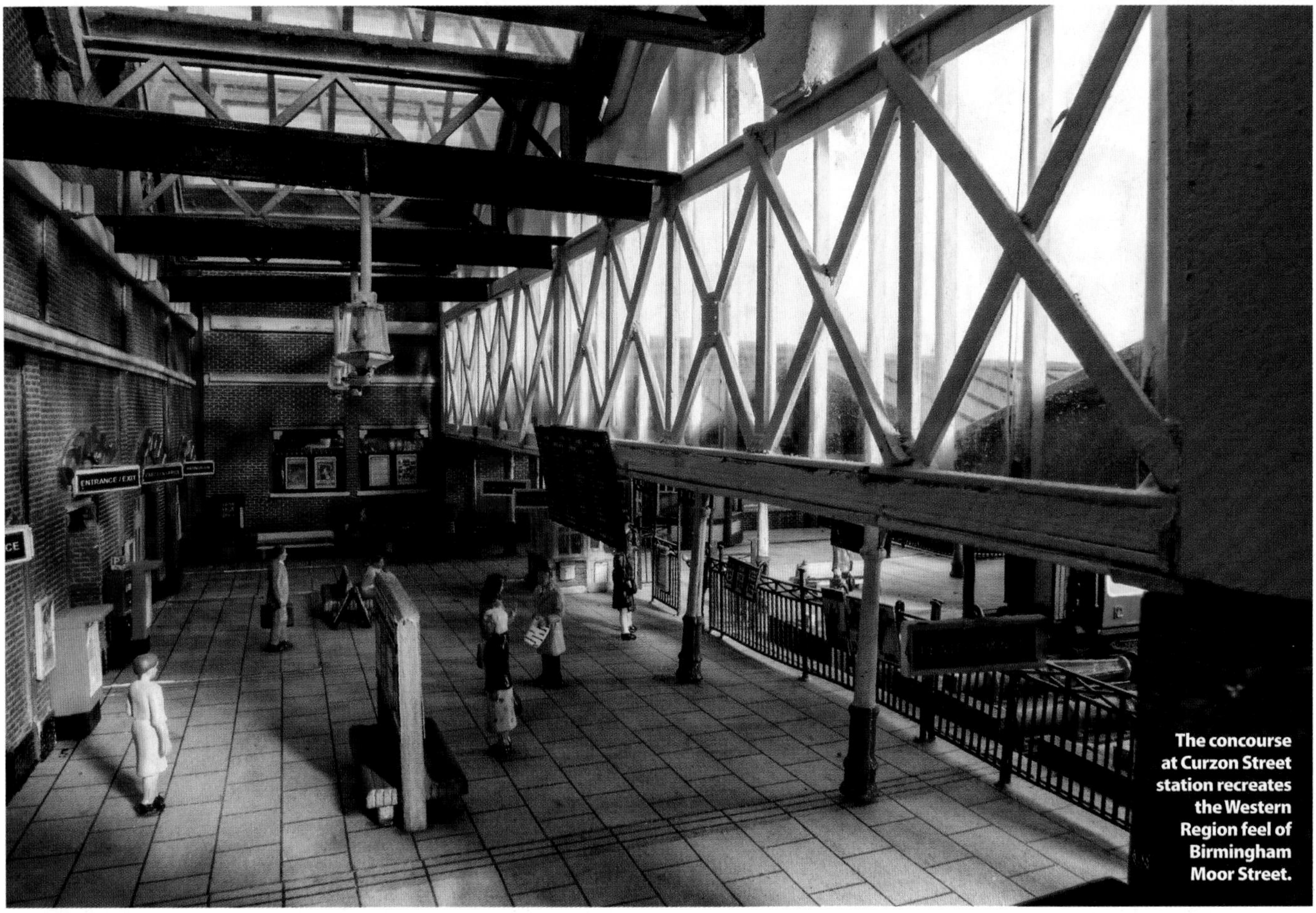

The concourse at Curzon Street station recreates the Western Region feel of Birmingham Moor Street.

THERE WILL be many readers who will empathise with Mark Wilson's modelling experience: "I started a number of layouts, but inspiration ran out before they were finished."

What he came to realise, "the hard way", was that his interest in multiple eras and locations was "the problem".

"This has, after many years of searching and planning, resulted in a multi-era, multi-location model that keeps me interested."

Penmouth and Curzon Street was inspired by Mark's happy memories, harking right back to being a seven-year-old enthusiast in 1977.

"I wanted to run and represent train movements of the Midlands, London, Cornwall and Devon. Having spent many hours at Birmingham New Street, for me the most interesting and unusual workings were trains to and from the South West.

"The challenge was to give a representation of the three areas so that, at first glance, other people seeing them would be able to take a good guess at the locations."

"A multi-era, multi-location model that keeps me interested."
MARK WILSON

The result? A 'somewhere to somewhere' layout, with a slice of 'somewhere' in between! »

PENMOUTH AND CURZON STREET TRACK DIAGRAM (Not to scale)

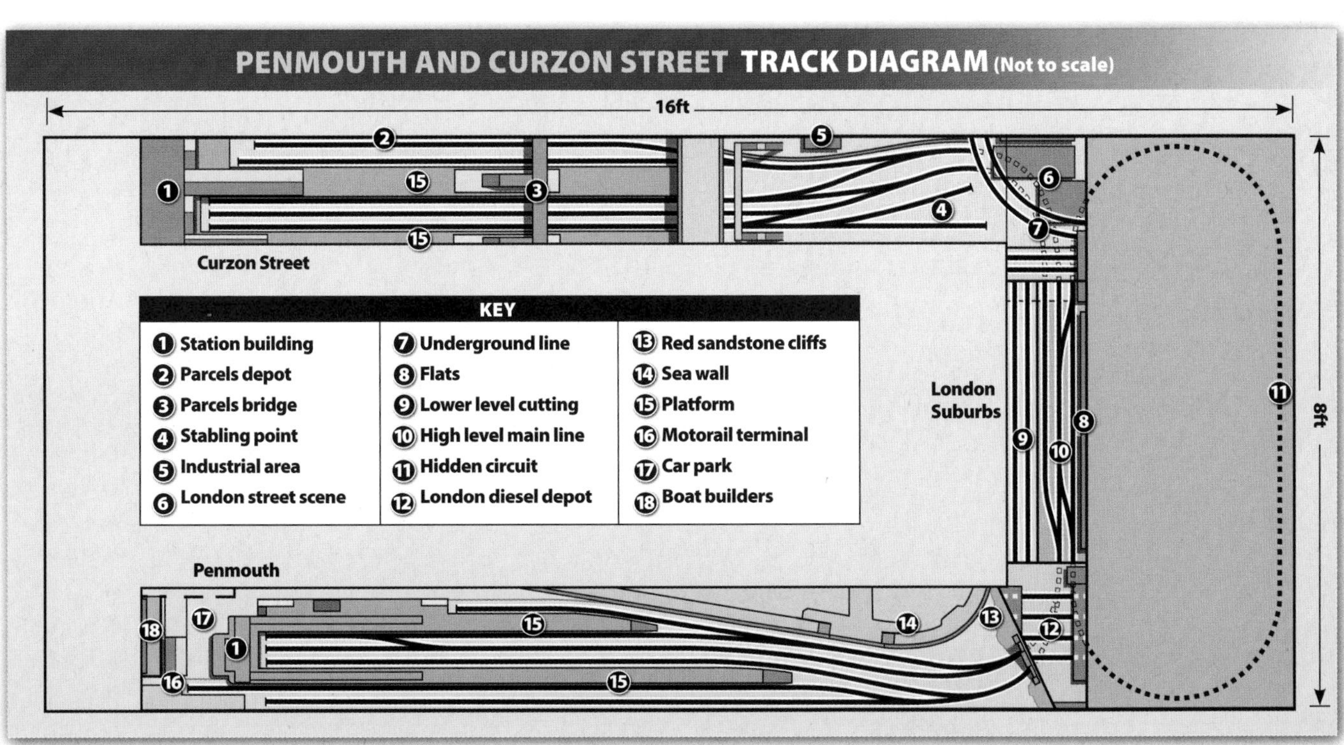

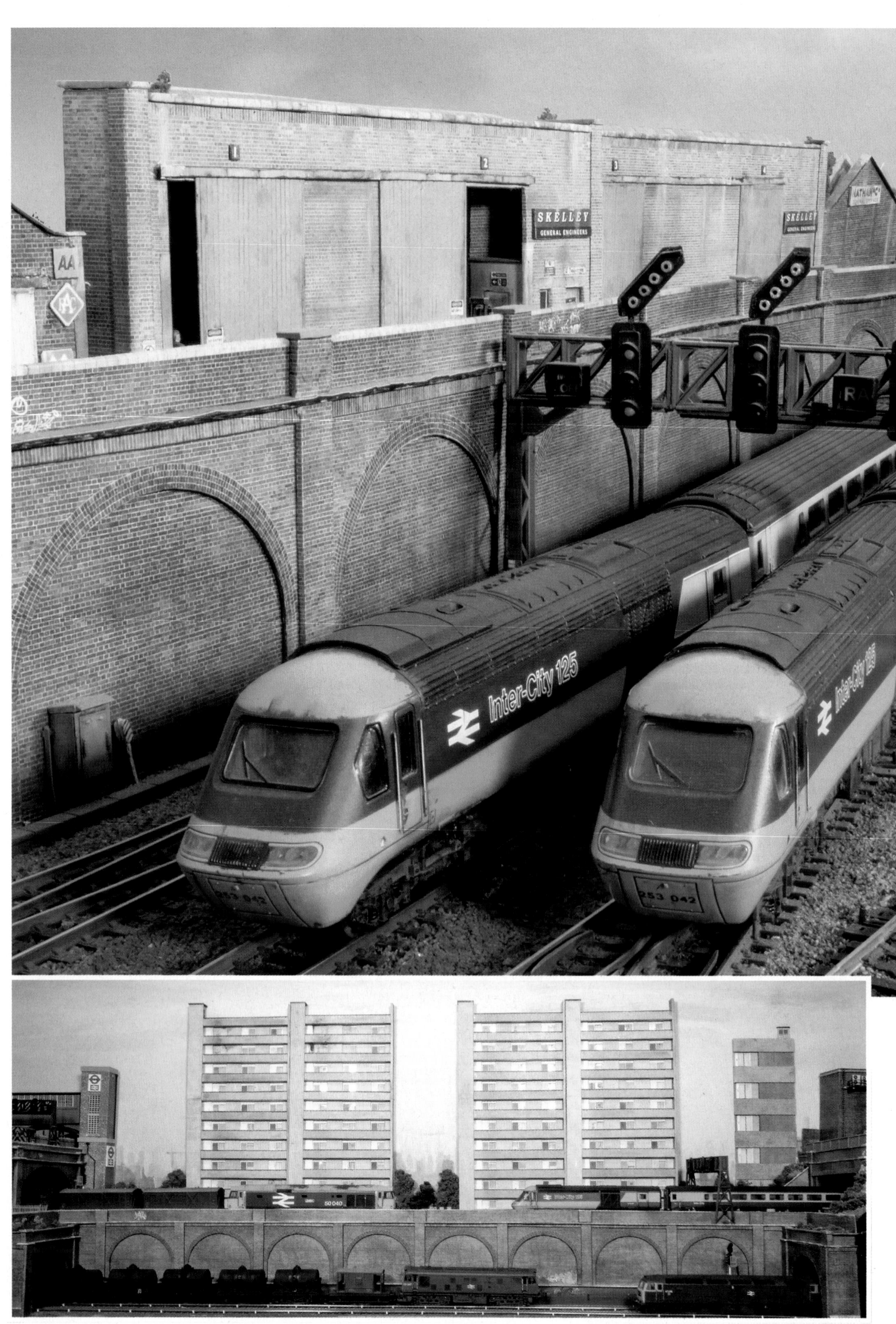
SKELLEY
GENERAL ENGINEERS
AA
Inter-City 125
253 042
50040

Cityscape...

The urban terminus, Curzon Street, is inspired by Birmingham Moor Street, with a few other nostalgic details included, like the parcel bridge, inspired by the one at Bristol Temple Meads, and the road bridge, which has echoes of Manchester Victoria Corporation Street.

The hemmed-in nature of the station throat is emphasised by the retaining wall and remains of a cramped ex-steam shed, now being used by the diesel crews as a wind break. Above is a typical industrial area with a small garage and warehouse buildings.

The middle section is modelled on the approaches to the capital with multiple routes crossing each other.

It starts in the left-hand corner with a typical street scene framed by a disused railway bridge against the backdrop. One side of the road has a cinema and a department store housed in art deco style buildings. Nearby is a typical London Underground station with its towers, signage and overbridge. The diorama tracks at high level represent the Underground and third-rail lines. These bridges have mirrors at the rear to create a sense of depth.

If you are reading *Great Layouts 4* from the front, you will already be familiar with Mark's virtuoso Spirit of Swindon, deploying similar devices that give the impression of grand space in a small area.

This low-relief section has a three-track main line with signal gantries to represent the approaches to the capital, with a dummy section of third-rail Southern Region double track disappearing into (dead-end!) tunnels at either end.

Continuing round the U-shaped run, another corner filler sees a locomotive depot with a waft of Finsbury Park: a six-road building with details including a fuel point, general stores and tanks. The retaining wall is made up of a mixture of brick finishes to give the feeling of different periods where walls have been added to over time.

As well as adding yet more scenic interest, this area doubles-up as another storage area for locomotives when they are not required on the layout. »

Above: **HSTs pass on the approach to Curzon Street while a Class 25 and 50 tick over at the servicing point.**

Opposite: **The layout design includes a continuous run circuit linked into the 'London Suburbs' section which allows locomotives to stretch their legs. A Birmingham-bound HST passes a Class 50 hauled parcels on the main line while on the electrified third-rail section, a Class 25 powered milk train crosses a Class 47 (in reality this cutting section is a non-powered diorama).**

Right: **Filling one corner of the layout and disguising the join between the London Suburbs and scenic Devon is a depot scene. This is used to store locomotives which aren't in use and today plays host to a Class 55 'Deltic' and a Class 08 shunter.**

Left: **A Motorail terminal has been modelled at Penmouth including the arrival terminal. The Beetle has arrived for the 10.35am to Newcastle.**

... Landscape

Unless trains are diverted into the hidden circuit (located under a stairwell), main line services take a Narnia-like entrance into the South West and the red cliffs of Devon Sea Wall, with the standout features Parsons Tunnel and Dawlish beach.

The railway passes over the path that leads down to the sea front with its walls, railings, fishing boats, nets, seagulls ("lurking around for the odd chip or snack"), beach huts and scattered rocks.

The railway terminates at Penmouth which has a strong flavour of the Great Western Main Line's terminus in Penzance, Cornwall. The overall roof is an extended Peco kit, sheltering three of the lengthy platforms. There is also a bay platform and a wall-side track that ends at the Motorail platform end, which also stores coaching stock for the sleeper service.

In front of the station building entrance is a vehicle turning area and taxi rank leading

Devon delight! South West holidays of yore are vividly recalled at the entrance to Penmouth as 'Class 31' 31402 rolls in.

A pair of Class 47s stand side-by-side Under the trainshed at Penmouth while tickets are checked at the barrier.

into the Motorail entrance booking-in shed and reception buildings. The latter buildings are based on those at Kensington Olympia, plus sections of canopy and a small loading ramp with white picket style gates, similar to that at Penzance from the 1960s to the 1980s.

"I made a point of building removable sections at the stations so that good camera angles have been created," Mark explains, "and therefore it can be looked through at barrier/fence height to give the views I remember growing up."

Through the ages

Traffic is formed of local, regional and long-distance trains plus parcels, perishables and when operating in early periods, milk and van traffic. Trains depart one station, loop around the central London section and then head either to Curzon Street or Penmouth, depending on where they started from.

The layout can currently operate through three different specific time periods: 1968-1972, 1972–1976 and 1977-1982 (the era featured on these pages). Each has its own timetable and rolling stock changes that slowly blend into one another, just as the real railway did.

"This allows me to transform maroon locomotives and coaching stock into the BR blue period ending in the popular 'large logo' livery," says Mark. "I am now in the process of adding two more periods – 1964-1968, allowing for the end of stea and the early green diesels with chocolate and cream Western Region coaching stock, and 1982-1986, for the beginning of the Network SouthEast and InterCity 'Swallow' liveries.

The mix of Ratio lower quadrants semaphores and Knightwing colour light signals are all removable and can be swapped around depending on what period is being represented.

Although Mark admits that Penmouth and Curzon Street "has taken a long time to come to fruition and a lot of work, it still gives me great enjoyment".

And that is, surely, what the hobby is all about. ■

READ MORE

Visit www.keymodelworld.com

Penmouth station is a combination of Peco overall roof and Scalescenes kits to create a large structure with strong echoes of Penzance.

Newpool-on-Trent

There's no limit to **GRAHAM TAYLOR's** modelling ambitions and imagination. Luckily, he had plenty of room to devise and build this bustling, complex reflection of Midlands steam in the Sixties.

PHOTOGRAPHY, MIKE WILD

The route to Gravelli crosses the main station at Newpool-on-Trent at right angles. Collett 4-6-0 7034 *Ince Castle* runs non-stop through the main line station as 5660 departs Gravelli above with some cattle vans.

The ungainly Caprotti valve gear fitted Stanier '5MT' 44756 passes beneath the streel-frame mounted signalbox.

It's the classic childhood dream. What started with a Triang *Princess Elizabeth* train set has mushroomed into a multi-station, multi-level epic layout with more than 50 locomotives.

Graham Taylor's love affair with railways is pretty typical for a boy growing up in the North West of the 1960s. For the young lad, it was shed bunks of Manchester's Longsight shed, spotting a wealth of 'namers' such as 'Patriots', 'Jubilees', 'Royal Scots' that really lit the flame.

"This gave me a love of the London Midland & Scottish Railway, and trips to Wales with my parents for holidays gave me a passion for the Great Western Railway."

Little surprise then that his ultimate modelling work draws heavily on both influences.

Newpool-on-Trent (Change for Gravalli and Capel Road) is a fictitious location somewhere in the Midlands where the former LMS and GWR met. Gravalli and Capel Road are the Western Region stations on the layout, while Newpool-on-Trent is mainly London Midland.

"Gravalli is made up from my name Graham and my wife's name Vaerie, and a LI on the end to give a Welsh name, Gravalli."

> *"I just run trains for the joy of seeing them moving."*
>
> **GRAHAM TAYLOR**

Up, down, round and round

The layout is housed in a room on ground level in a former police station, adjoining the couple's house.

The double track forms a large oval with four roads through the main station, Newpool-on-Trent, where there is a bay platform and goods yard on the Down side.

This is served by a six-road locomotive shed with an impressive allocation of 55 engines. A (Heljan) turntable, sanding plant, lifting hoist, concrete coaling tower and ash plant complete the large depot.

Opposite the station there is a 17-road storage yard, nine lines of which can hold eight-coach trains.

Gravalli, the branch terminus, includes a bay for an autotrain, goods yard and timber yard and single road engine shed. This is at a higher level than the main line and crosses at right angles via a girder bridge over the platforms of the main line station. The line then follows the main line from where it disappears into the hidden storage yard while on a falling gradient to reach a platform at Newpool-on-Trent station.

Another branch veers away from Newpool in the opposite direction to Capel Road, featuring a bay for an autotrain, goods yard, single road engine shed and private siding to a dairy. »

A triumph of drive and ambition. All three stations can just be seen in this extraordinary view of Graham Taylor's dedicated railway room.

Right: **At Capel Road, GWR '45XX' 2-6-2T 4569 rolls to a stop with a 'B-set' while a Hunslet 'Austerity' shunts wagons from the dairy.**

Below: **Rebuilt 'Royal Scot' 4-6-0 46102 *Black Watch* leads a Travelling Post Office train on the main line as a GWR '56XX' 0-6-2T crosses above on the branch to Newpool with a rake of cattle wagons.**

This country outpost is reached via a gradient on a baseboard above the storage yard. This was also a terminus, until one of Graham's close friends, and professional railwayman, Bob Hart provided inspiration for how the run could be extended further.

One of Bob's suggestions was to extend the line at Capel Road to make it a through station and join up with the line coming out of Gravalli.

"Now I had an end to end run from Gravalli to Capel Road via Newpool-on-Trent where the configuration of points allowed the branch to crossover to the main line."

Bob's next agreeable suggestion was to add a left-hand chord at the exit to Gravelli to join the continuous loop close to Capel Road to form a triangle, which can also be used to turn locomotives as part of the run-round procedure at Gravalli.

Bob, a main line steam traction inspector, "has seen the progress of my construction on a weekly basis and has been like a technical advisor to me during the build," adds Graham.

"His experience of the 'big railway' has been invaluable."

Lights... action

The layout is analogue with four control panels, indicated by the track plan which is broken into colour coded sections. Each has a switch to either isolate it or select which cab (controller) to use.

With the storage yard being hidden by the baseboard for Capel Road on top of it, route setting is confirmed using point indicators supplied by Heathcote Electronics. That company's Infrared Detection of Trains is used to indicate which storage yard tracks are occupied with LEDs.

Signals are a mixture of three-aspect colour lights for the main lines and upper quadrant (LMS) semaphores, while the branch lines showcase classic GWR lower quadrants.

For Graham, there is no rigid timetable: "I don't have an operating procedure yet, as most of my time has been spent on building the layout. At present, I just run trains for the joy of seeing them moving."

The locomotive fleet includes 58 LMS, 25 GWR, 23 London, North Eastern Railway, 10 Southern Railway, and 16 BR Standard »

NEWPOOL-ON-TRENT TRACK DIAGRAM (Not to scale)

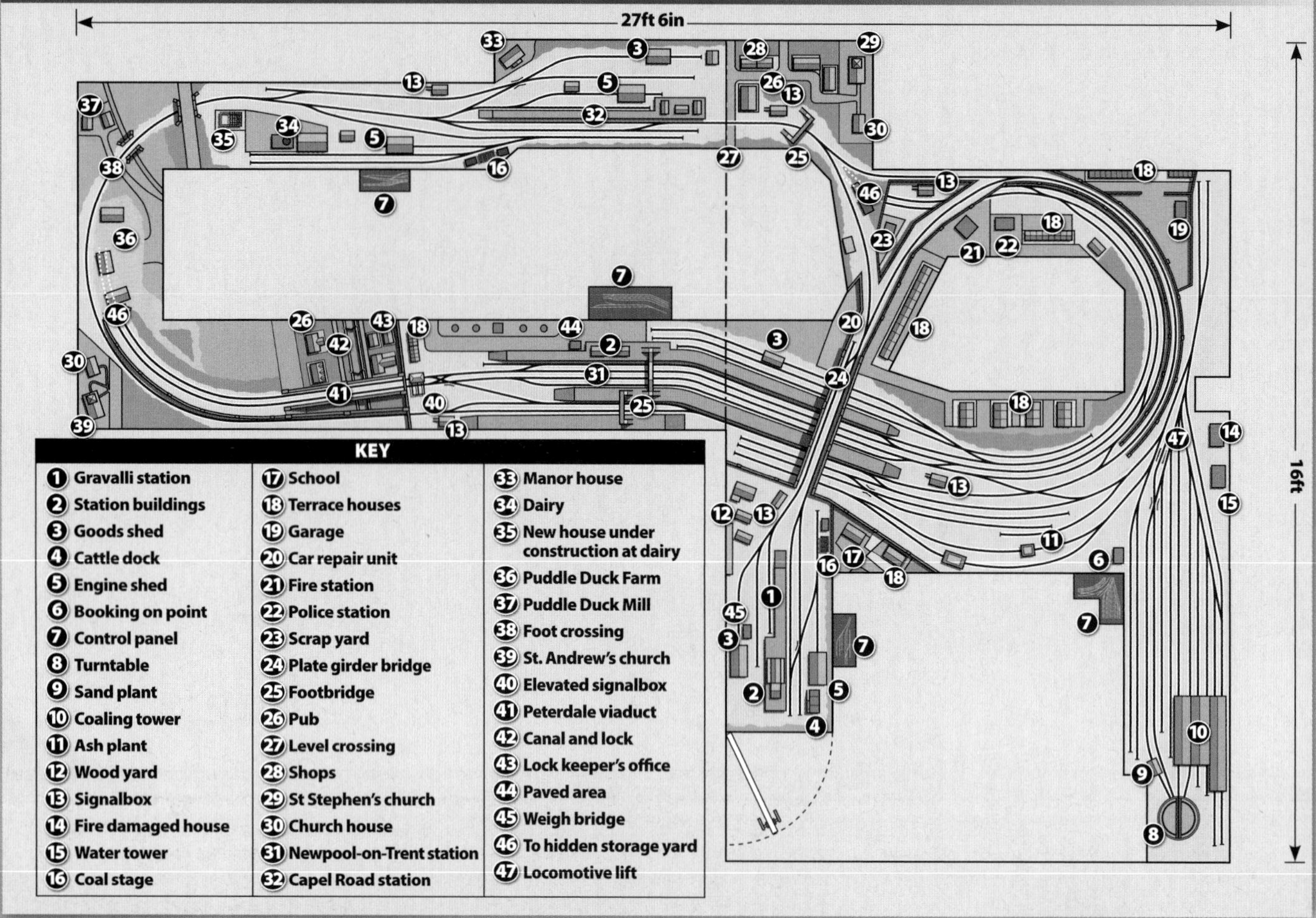

27ft 6in

16ft

KEY

1. Gravalli station
2. Station buildings
3. Goods shed
4. Cattle dock
5. Engine shed
6. Booking on point
7. Control panel
8. Turntable
9. Sand plant
10. Coaling tower
11. Ash plant
12. Wood yard
13. Signalbox
14. Fire damaged house
15. Water tower
16. Coal stage
17. School
18. Terrace houses
19. Garage
20. Car repair unit
21. Fire station
22. Police station
23. Scrap yard
24. Plate girder bridge
25. Footbridge
26. Pub
27. Level crossing
28. Shops
29. St Stephen's church
30. Church house
31. Newpool-on-Trent station
32. Capel Road station
33. Manor house
34. Dairy
35. New house under construction at dairy
36. Puddle Duck Farm
37. Puddle Duck Mill
38. Foot crossing
39. St. Andrew's church
40. Elevated signalbox
41. Peterdale viaduct
42. Canal and lock
43. Lock keeper's office
44. Paved area
45. Weigh bridge
46. To hidden storage yard
47. Locomotive lift

Monstrous LMS Garratt 47981 and Crosti '9F' 92029 are disposed of on Newpool shed as 46521 *City of Nottingham* rattles along the main line with an express.

steam locomotives, with diesels consisting of a 'Midland Pullman' and 'Derby Lightweight' diesel multiple unit.

Buildings are out of the box Hornby Skaledale or Bachmann Scenecraft to save build time, although canopies are Dapol and Ratio kits positioned on Wills embossed paving platforms.

The large signalbox at Newpool-on-Trent station was made by gluing two Hornby 'boxes together (with the steps removed from one), while another on the main line has been adapted by sitting on top of Plastruct steel girders.

The long plate girder bridge which passes over the main line for Gravalli station is also made from plastic steel components.

There is only space to mention a fraction of the other infrastructure features, namely the canal with lock under Peterdale Viaduct and a wedding taking places at St Andrew's Parish Church. At Capel Road stands another church, St Stephen's.

In the town area are rows of terraced houses, a police station and fire station. A garage is to be found under one of the railway high level arches where blue flashes reveal that an arc welding set is being used.

In total there are 70 working street, platform and yard lights (supplied by Layouts 4U).

"A railway is never finished," Graham contemplates. "I want to weather more of the locomotives and rolling stock, having only done a few to date. I also intend to add crew and lights to locomotives, plus lots of other little tasks.

"The experience of building a large layout has been wonderful. I have learnt a lot about the hobby and am proud of what I have achieved." ■

READ MORE

Visit www.keymodelworld.com

Above: **'Black Five' 44756 crosses Peterdale Viadcut with an express as a GWR '64XX' 0-6-0PT leads an autotrain on the gradient to the upper level Western Region branch line.**

Original condition 'Baby Scot' or 'Patriot' 45503 *The Royal Leicestershire Regiment* hurries through the middle roads at Newpool-on-Trent with a fitted van train.

North Cornwall Brewery

Cornwall's breweries are known across the land… **MALCOLM BRIGGS** reveals one of its much lesser-known examples in a pretty corner of its north coast.

PHOTOGRAPHY, MIKE WILD

Ford Transits line the yard as the Hunslet 'Austerity' propels a rake of vans for loading and a Drummond '700' waits to leave with its brake van.

YOU HAVE probably heard of the North Cornwall Railway and its famous 'Atlantic Coast Express' to Padstow. But did you know its metals also served a brewery in Knight's Hill near Camelford?

No? That's because, of course, they actually didn't. Indeed, Knight's Hill doesn't exist. But let yourself be indulged in Malcolm Briggs' imagination for a moment.

In his 4mm:1ft world, the North Cornwall Brewery was opened in the 1850s at the point where the ample-flowing River Allen crossed the turnpike that eventually became the A39 or 'Atlantic Highway'. That meant the brewery had access to an ample source of water and a horse-drawn means to serve the sparsely-populated rural parts of North Cornwall as well as towns as far apart as Liskeard and Launceston. However, most of the produce was taken to Port Isaac where coastal sailing ships took it around the Cornwall and Devon coast.

A Ford Thames is loaded with barrels at the dock.

Sea, rail and road

Yet when the Great Western Railway connected to the Bodmin & Wadebridge Railway in the 1880s, the brewery operation was transformed. Suddenly, it could take beer to Bodmin by horse, from where it could reach London by rail – the same day. The sailing ships were soon dismissed.

When the London, South Western Railway finally decided to reach the North Cornish coast in the 1870s, the brewery's directors lobbied hard for the route to come sufficiently close to enable them to develop an internal system connected to the national network.

Expansion followed throughout the 20th Century until we reach the 1960s where BR Southern Region steam is just hanging on in this backwater and the brewery is once again thinking about modernisation, by utilising road transport. Barley and hops grown in Somerset and Worcestershire are beginning to arrive in large lorries, not just in sacks in open four-wheel railway wagons…

For now, being connected to the network means that trains still arrive from direct from BR and enter the main arrival/departure line. The locomotive is uncoupled and it runs around to collect the brake van and then sets off back to the main line at Knight's Hill station. One of the brewery company's two locomotives then shunts the wagons – coals to the power station, timber to the cooperage and barley to the unloading bay. »

"Some parts I have absolutely hated and couldn't wait to be over."

MALCOLM BRIGGS

Knight's night... Activity at the brewery entrance continues into the evening.

Once unloaded, fresh trains are then marshalled with loaded open and more usually, closed wagons full of barrels and then they are taken to the exchange sidings (off-scene) so that they can be taken back down the branch when BR come to collect them.

Being a private railway with BR operating rights means that certain aspects do not have to meet Board of Trade requirements – there are no shunting signals, for example, and there is no requirement to run passenger trains, although a DMU does arrive morning and evening to run to the bay platform at Knight's Hill for the workers.

Bespoke buildings

Okay, so that's the background. What about the layout that this fictional history stimulated in Malcom's mind's eye?

His previous layout had taken 30 years to build, while professing a love for making buildings, "but because this was meant to be a quick build, I went for large industrial units in a range of styles that demonstrated their age of construction".

Clockwise from the brewery entrance, the buildings are:

Head Office: Constructed in the 1850s, it was also the main brewery in the early days, set around a small quadrangle which has now been roofed over and a cupola installed. If the front wall looks like the STEAM museum in Swindon, don't be surprised, as Bachmann offered a resin model of it and it is very similar to the Elgood's brewery in Wisbech. The primary difference from Elgood's is that the North Cornwall Brewery is built in stone, not brick.

Brewery malting: Built in the late 1800s, it is now used for bottling of lager, keg beers and other minority drinks. The pipes that come from the modern factory carry this fizzy concoction are made from plastic sheet with Wills windows and arches. The roof of this building and the Head Office are covered in tile paper.

Loading bay: Built around the turn of the century, it shows signs of much modification over the years. It is also fully detailed inside and lit.

Cooperage: This is a post-war building as the original burned down and it is where the barrels are made. It is constructed from plastic sheet throughout.

A new house is under construction in the village. Malcolm built this scene from individual bricks – a painstaking but worthwhile process. Just look at it!

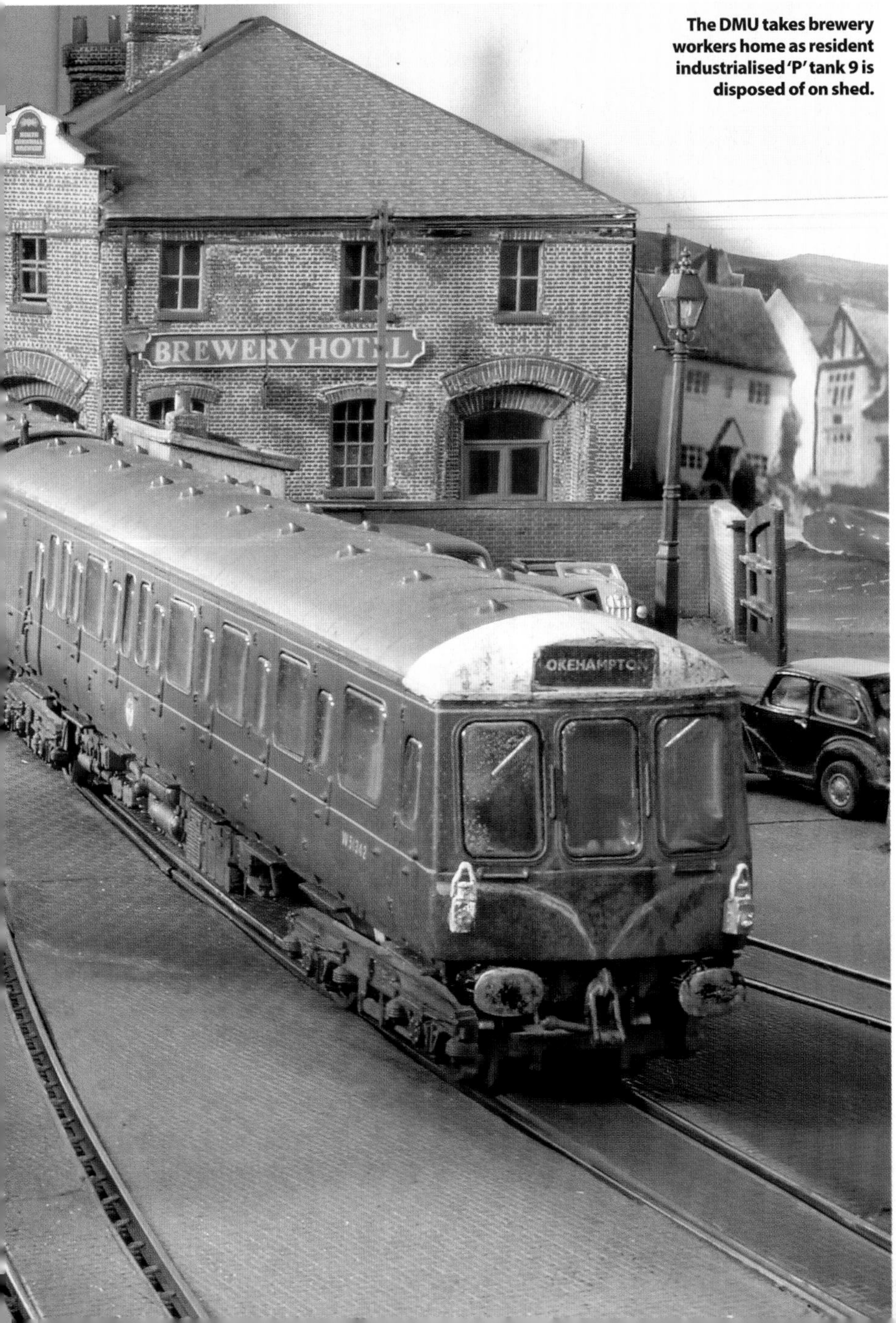

The DMU takes brewery workers home as resident industrialised 'P' tank 9 is disposed of on shed.

Modern factory: Built in the 1930s, this is a modernist building which balances the twee nature of the earlier buildings. It is all Plastikard and with a representation of the modern brewery inside, which is mostly only visible when the lights are on.

Power house: This is based on one small wing of the Crossness Pumping Station. It is multi-layered plastic sheet building with Wills windows and L-Cut roofing tile strips. It contains full internal detail comprising stationary boiler, control desk, turbine, coal storage and pipework.

Motor transport depot: This cameo is all made from odds and ends of Plastikard and Evergreen girders.

Engine shed: This is just big enough to take two small engines and with full interior detail and lighting; all constructed from plastic sheets.

Various bothies: There's a toilet block, a weighbridge station, two security boxes and a train control box. Most are in brewery style whereas the train control box is brutalist concrete. All were made from plastic sheets.

In the adjacent village, there are a host of highly detailed buildings, including Brewery Cottages, two bungalows, a tin Methodist church, a Post Office, a butcher's and a fish & chip shop. This has a genuine art deco interior and fish fryer, complete with queue of people standing outside.

Theatrical performance

"Being involved in both the exhibition industry and backstage for an amateur dramatic group means that I have an interest in presenting displays or exhibits in a way that is visually attractive as well as being more akin to a theatrical performance," says Malcolm.

"This means we only operate the layout from the back at shows and the visitor should not be more than marginally aware of the operators, although we do try to ensure someone is out front answering questions." »

NORTH CORNWALL BREWERY TRACK DIAGRAM (Not to scale)
16ft
2ft
Storage yard
Storage yard
KEY
1 Knight's Hill village
2 Car garage
3 House under construction
4 Level crossing
5 Public house
6 Engine shed
7 Brewery headquarters
8 Bottling plant
9 Loading dock
10 Cooperage
11 Loading point
12 Barrel run
13 Factory
14 Power house
15 Vehicle maintenance
33009

In order to achieve this, he has constructed something akin to a stage, with wings, fascia and proscenium arch. The overall curved roof of the layout contains LED lighting, which is configured like stage lighting so that the time of day and even the season can be simulated. As night falls on the layout and hundreds of lights come on in both the brewery and the surrounding village.

"I've really enjoyed some parts of building this layout and didn't want it to finish," he reflects. "Some parts I have absolutely hated and couldn't wait to be over, but that's modelling life for you!"

We couldn't agree more... and we'll certainly drink to that, Malcolm. Cheers! ■

READ MORE

Visit www.keymodelworld.com

Above: **The aroma of beer battered cod has wafted across Knight's Hill... No surprise that a queue has gathered at the chip shop.**

Right: **The street scenes are every bit as interesting as the railway operations. At Knight's Hill hardware store the local decorator has collected a fresh roll of carpet for his latest project.**

Left: **Bulleid 'Q1' 0-6-0 33009 couples up to a loaded rake of wagons for departure from the North Cornwall Brewery.**

Old Elm Park

'O' gauge layouts usually take up a lot of room, but **MARK POLLARD** proves that you can mix big locomotives with modest space as he welcomes us inside his atmospheric roundhouse.

PHOTOGRAPHY, TREVOR JONES

It was a photograph that "really got the imagination going". Mark Pollard was perusing a copy of the *Great Western Echo*, a society magazine for members of Didcot Railway Centre, when a double page picture of Old Oak Common roundhouse leapt out.

"The idea was born to build a layout as if you are standing in the building looking at the turntable with locomotives stabled around the shed... simmering and bubbling away."

Conveniently, this design would also allow Mark somewhere to display a large number of his extensive collection of locomotives.

"Ideas began going through my mind while studying various books, photographs and websites were all about detail and atmosphere, dull lighting and creating the atmosphere of a working steam shed."

'O' gauge is usually associated with space-soaking layouts, but Mark was able to squeeze Old Elm Park into just 8ft square.

"This really is minimum space modelling 'O' gauge," he affirms. "To convey the shed atmosphere that I wanted I set it nearly 5ft off the ground to give viewers eye-level viewing into the roundhouse."

A Drummond 'M7' 0-4-4T eases off the turntable on arrival at the depot.

Self-contained

Baseboards were made from a kit of parts cut by B&Q, resulting in a robust structure with a viewing window on the front edge. The layout is of the self-contained with the roof being an integral part of the cameo.

There are two boxes 4ft wide; one 32in deep and one 16in deep, the larger which accommodates the turntable.

The wheel arches in Mark's car can just about fit the larger of the two boards so the layout can be taken to exhibitions. The roof is removable in two sections and the girder work made from plastic strip, thin timber, brass and plastic rod.

The turntable is from a Kitwood Models kit, which in Mark's experience "made up very easily, runs well and is affordable". The pit was cut out of the baseboard with a jigsaw. The roof is made from thin MDF finished with smoke chutes from plastic electric trunking, while the truss and girder work is made from plastic and strip wood parts.

SCALE	GAUGE	SIZE	PERIOD	CONTROL
7mm:1ft	'O', 32mm	4ft x 4ft	1960s	DCC, Lenz 100

OLD ELM PARK TRACK DIAGRAM (Not to scale)

4ft

4ft

1 2 3 4 4 4 5 5 5

KEY

1. Entrance
2. Viewing side
3. Turntable
4. Diesels only
5. Storage lines

"My wife says it needs a shed small so if anyone has any ideas...."

MARK POLLARD

Below: **Old Elm Park roundhouse scene occupies just 4ft square and yet the sense of space is awe-inspiring.**

Fitters attend to GWR '5205' 2-8-0T 5223 ensuring it is ready for its next goods service.

Track is all made from C+L Finescale components with the chairs being laid on the shed floor without slopes as inset and pits cut out of the baseboard.

Depending on the size of locomotives, nearly 30 can be stabled in the shed at one time.

Many of the cameo scenes around the shed are made up from spare detail parts from various suppliers and parts kit leftovers.

All figures are from the Modelu 3D printed range along with the standpipes and 'bashed' barrels and stepladders from Invertrain.

Mark used a mix of weathering powders, paints dry brushed and weathering products from various suppliers to get the effect of oil, water, ash and general grime on the shed floor and walls.

To generate a suitable dingy working shed atmosphere, lighting is all LEDs hidden in the roof supports.

Collett '57XX' 0-6-0PT 6737 moves onto the turntable. The sprawling shed roads can hold up to 30 locomotives!

Western, Southern and Midland region motive power rubs shoulders at Old Elms Park. Figures are from the Modelu 3D printed range.

Fictional reality

In order to justify the sizeable collection of Southern Railway and GWR locomotives, a fictional reality was executed – Old Elm Park was a roundhouse built just outside Reading.

It was developed when the rival companies began to share facilities for combined operations at Reading General station and provided motive power for services to the south coast via Basingstoke, Redhill or into south west London.

The fleet includes a large number of kit built Western and Southern region motive power as well as recent ready-to-run products that regular readers will recognise.

These include Dapol '57XX' and '64XX' 0-6-0PTs, Heljan Class 33 and 42, a Minerva Models '8750' 0-6-0PT and others.

Kit built locomotives regularly seen on the layout include a GWR '14XX' 0-4-2T, '1500' 0-6-0PT, '47XX' 2-8-0 and '5205' 2-8-0T, LSWR Drummond 'M7' 0-4-4T, SECR Maunsell 'N' 2-6-0 and Southern Bulleid 'Q1' 0-6-0, LMS '8F' 2-8-0 and a BR '9F' 2-10-0, though other classes make appearances too, having uncoupled from inter regional services heading north or south.

With a simple 'fiddle stick' - basically a plug in cassette that connects to the entrance/exit road - locomotives can be sent to the turntable and redirected to a storage track while waiting their next turn of duty.

The turntable runs nice and slowly from its DCC Gaugemaster controller and is lined up by eye.

"This layout is all about atmosphere," Mark asserts. With full DCC sound, the echoes of a steam shed "fill the air".

"My wife says it needs a shed smell so if anyone has any ideas..." ■

READ MORE

Visit www.keymodelworld.com

Oak Road

An all-action Great Western Main Line scene is the result of **MIKE BUICK's** modelling endeavors. But this exhibition cracker also has a bigger role to play by supporting the charitable work of Meningitis Now.

PHOTOGRAPHY, RICHARD WATSON

A pair of GWR Class 800 bi-mode five-car units glide through Oak Road. In the yard, 66068 is now ready to depart with its IOA wagons while a Class 153 and 150 stand in multiple in the bay platform.

A Class 153 scurries away from Oak Road on the branch line as a Freightliner operated Class 66 passes under the road bridge with a rake of empty Network Rail 'Falcon' ballast wagons.

HOW MANY times have you been to an exhibition and heard a child enquire, 'why aren't there any trains moving?'

It was that potential threat of boredom that inspired the construction, and exhibition, of Oak Road. Its creator, Mike Buick, wanted to appeal to a wide audience, one that encompassed fast, brightly coloured trains, for the younger viewers, while attaining a modelling standard approving of the seasoned viewer.

"Given the fact that I could barely build an Airfix kit before I started out, nor had the skill or understanding to build a finescale model railway to 'P4' standards," wasn't the most auspicious of starts to his adventure. Undeterred, Mike took heart from Pete Goss's World's End "which looked the part" employing Peco code 75 track and re-spaced the sleepers to give a more realistic appearance, but still enabling ready-to-go 'OO' gauge stock to run.

Naturally, he decided to follow the same process, as well as incorporating superelevated curves. This was achieved by building up strips of paper stuck down with PVA glue under the outer edge of the sleepers.

The station building is the Ratio kit based on the GWR's Castle Cary, prompting Mike to go and see what it looked like in real life.

"This provided me with ideas for the scenery and the final fictitious location in the Somerset village of Lyttle Cary which serves the lines to Taunton and Weymouth to the west, and Westbury and Shepton Mallet (long gone in real life) to the east."

> *"Whenever we're at shows, myself and the operating team raise as much money as we can to help support Meningitis research."*
>
> **MIKE BUICK**

Castle build

The station is the main feature of the layout and although mine isn't actually replica of Castle Cary, there are a few references to the real location, such as the footbridge (made using 'bashed' parts from a couple readily available kits).

The platforms were made using Peco platform edging covered with Slaters embossed brick sheet, and foamboard bracing added to support the tops, which are a combination of Slaters embossed paving and scored plasticard. These were painted using acrylics.

The station lights are scratchbuilt too, using lanterns that Alan Buttler of Modelu 3D-printed, and the station signage is courtesy of Steve Bell at Railtec. Scale Model Scenery made the bespoke palisade fencing for the station car park, as well as the chain link fence that follows the lineside.

The colour light signals were built by Paul Folds of CR Signals for the layout and are exact replicas of the westbound signal at Castle Cary, while the ground signals came from Matt Turner at Absolute Aspects. »

The tunnel is a replica of Somerton Tunnel's eastern portal, which again was scratch-built ("three times because I just couldn't get it right"), as are the two road-over-rail bridges.

All of the roads are made using plasticard, again painted with acrylic paint.

The landscape is created using carved up polystyrene covered in torn up brown paper soaked in PVA, "and what a mess that made!", Mike recalls. The rock cutting is formed using toilet roll soaked in PVA and sculpted using a wallpaper scraper.

The stone yard doesn't exist at Castle Carey, but it is a useful space filler and is made in a similar way to the rest of the landscape, but using expanded foam as a basis, again covered in brown paper, PVA, and lots of ballast.

The track was ballasted using sieved Calsisand, available from Pets At Home, and originally intended for reptile vivariums. It is fixed with diluted Mod Podge glue.

Watered down burnt umber and black paint was applied to the track and ballast with a pipette which once dry leaves a dusty 'West Country finish'.

"There's very few static aspects of the layout which haven't been redone at some point, which personally, I feel adds to the realistic looking appearance," Mike explains. "After all, most roads have been dug-up and repaired throughout their lives; buildings are being redeveloped, built or demolished; and the railway is always being re-ballasted."

HST finale

James Hudson at DCC Train Automation supplied the Digikeijs DR5000 and a Piko

Class 158 158956 is ready to depart as a Class 800 sweeps under the stone arch bridge on the approach to the station.

> *"I could barely build an Airfix kit before I started out, nor had the skill or understanding to build a finescale model railway to 'P4' standards"*
>
> **MIKE BUICK**

Mendip Rail JNA wagons wait to be loaded at the stone sidings. 66101 idles in the yard between duties.

Throttle, providing Mike with the advantage of using a computer program called iTrain via Loconet.

"The benefit is that we could operate the layout manually or semi-automatically if we were talking to visitors at exhibitions. I can put it in to full automation when I'm sat at home and just watch the trains go by."

The Digikeijs system has since been expanded using other products in the Digikeijs range including DR4088 feedback modules to tell the computer system where the trains are on the layout, and DR4018 accessory modules to drive the point motors and the colour light signals.

The (fully-weathered) rolling stock which operates on Oak Road covers a six-year period on the Great Western section of the main line railway and sets the time frame between 2013 and 2019.

Adds Mike: "Highlights are undoubtedly the full-length High Sped Trains snaking through the station and I have amassed a selection of units in GWR green and First Great Western dynamic lines purple, as well as 'celebrity' power cars such as 43002 *Sir Kenneth Grange* in its final BR blue and yellow colour scheme as it was at the end of HST operation by GWR."

The HSTs are joined by a pair of Class 800 five-car bi-mode units and DMUs from classes 150, 153 and 158 all operate alongside the express workings.

Freight traffic is naturally in the hands of Class 66s in most cases, with examples in Freightliner, EWS and DB Schenker liveries. There are also DRS Class 37s and a West Coast Railways Class 47 while a Class 70 also makes occasional appearances. »

Class 43 43002 *Sir Kenneth Grange* leads an HST set into Oak Road. Note the HST stop signs at the platforms ends and the specially made single aspect modern LED signals.

DB Schenker liveried Class 66 66101 passes through Oak Road with a rake of china clay tankers. 3D printed models of layout owner Mike Buick and *Hornby Magazine's* Richard Watson look on.

GWR's uniquely liveried 43172 *Harry Patch* coasts through Oak Road as Class 66 66068 prepares to uncouple from its rake of IOA ballast box wagons in the yard. The Ratio station building takes centre stage on the platform.

OAK ROAD TRACK DIAGRAM (Not to scale)

KEY

1 Somerton Tunnel	4 Station approach	7 Virtual quarry	10 Footbridge
2 Road	5 Car garage unit	8 Platform	11 Bay Platform
3 Stone arched bridge	6 Virtual quarry sidings	9 Station building	12 Anson Road Bridge No. 1

Meningitis Now

In 1986, just before his 20th birthday, Mike contracted Meningococcal Meningitis.

"By all rights, should not be here to tell this story, let alone build a model railway (you can read my story at *oak-road.co.uk/my-story/*).

"I wondered if I could help someone else beat this terrible disease, so I contacted Meningitis Now and told them about my experience and how I had a big train set, and asked if I could raise some money? To my surprise, they said 'yes'.

"The charity sent me some T-shirts and a collection bucket... Whenever we're at shows, myself and the operating team raise as much money as we can to help support Meningitis research."

Tim Horn also made and donated a full-size replica nameplate from HST power car 43041 when it was named *Meningitis Trust Support For Life*, now fixed to the fascia board above the layout during shows.

Although Mike has built Oak Road on his own, he readily accepts that he could never have done it without help from many, many people, not least "the amazing doctors and nurses who saved my life, because without them, you would not be reading this now.

"Thank you so very, very much." ■

READ MORE

- Meningitis Now can be supported via Mike's just giving page www.justgiving.com/fundraising/mike-buick
- Visit www.keymodelworld.com

A GWR HST set headed by 43093 *Old Oak Common – HST Depot 1976-2018* rolls to a stop at Oak Road as another set departs in the opposite direction. The virtual quarry is loading up a trio of Mendip Rail JNA box wagons in the background while a Class 153 ticks over in the bay platform waiting for cross-platform passengers.

Lostwithiel

The Cornish main line station of Lostwithiel has been the subject of three layouts by **ROB ELLIOTT**. Here he reveals the full story behind this inspirational tail-chaser which encompasses the main line and the Fowey branch – all in a spare bedroom!

Palm trees and china clay-stained wagons are vital clues our location... it can only be sunny Cornwall! A 'Small Prairie' runs along the Up Main as the Fowey autotrain service waits in Lostwithiel's bay platform in the charge of a GWR 0-4-2T.

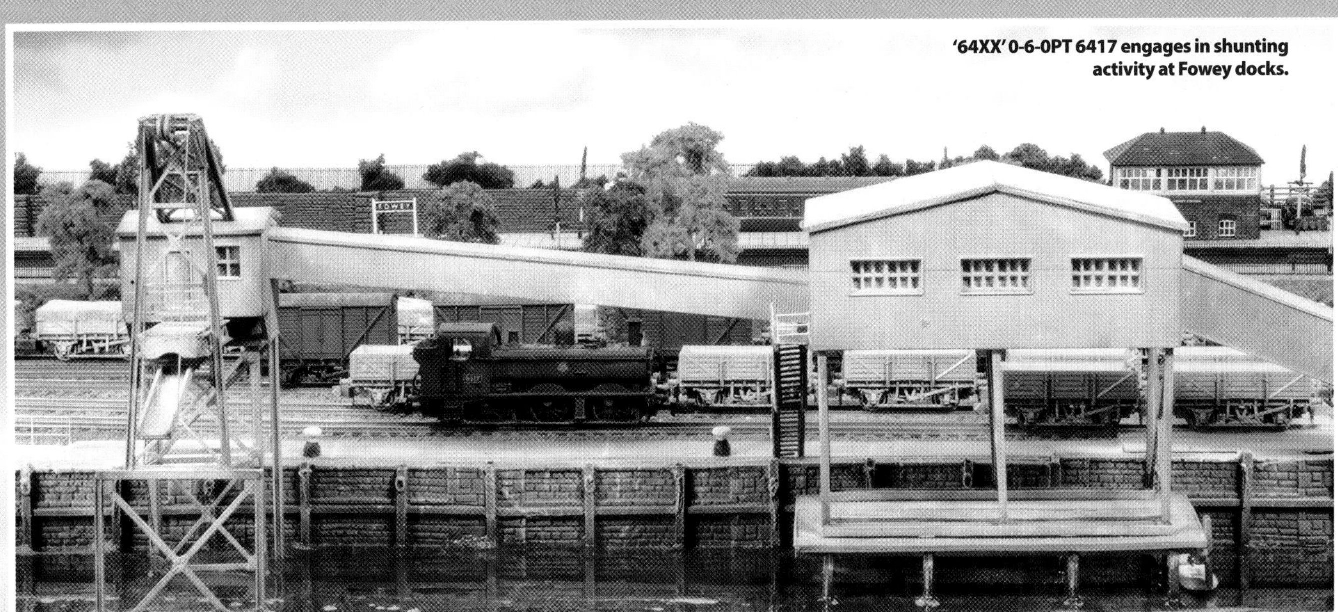

'64XX' 0-6-0PT 6417 engages in shunting activity at Fowey docks.

"When my wife and I were looking for our first house six years ago, one of the conditions was a spare room to house a permanent 'N' gauge layout and modelling desk. I was lucky enough that my wife agreed so long as she got a sewing room as well."

And so it was that the dream of a (third!) layout of Lostwithiel in Cornwall became a reality for Rob Elliott.

Work commenced converting one of the bedrooms (9ft x 9ft), painting the walls sky blue that was act as a simple, yet clean, backscene to the planned layout.

The aim was to represent Lostwithiel station, with its goods shed, dairy, crossing and adjacent sidings; the branch line to Fowey station incorporating Golant causeway and the clay docks at Carne Point; all stitched together by a continuous run double track main line with up and down goods loops for clay trains.

"It was an ambitious list," Rob admits, "but with 'N' gauge as the choice of scale, it was achievable in the space that I had available". »

The detailed plan suited all of his requirements to run interesting trains, including clay, parcels, milk, general goods and local/express passenger. There are several areas for shunting, an end-to-end element for local autotrain services between Lostwithiel and Fowey, and the aforementioned continuous circuit.

Unusually, Rob decided not to include a storage yard a it would have taken away the opportunity of a double-track main line running through countryside on a sweeping curve.

He reveals why the platforms aren't also curved, as per the prototype: "I soon realised that I would not be able to make a completely accurate model of the real place in the space, so compromises would need to be made. Including the curved platforms would mean removing a lot of pointwork and significantly shortening the loops."

Similar compromises have been made in the Fowey/Carne Point area, which are a representation rather than faithful reproduction.

The Right Tone

Once laid, wired up and thoroughly tested, the Peco Code 55 track was embedded with Woodland Scenics fine grey ballast, lightly sprayed with Humbrol brown aerosol and weathered using Tamiya acrylics through an airbrush.

Platforms are made from Peco platform edging, painted with a mix of dark browns and greys, allowed to dry and then lightly sanded with wet and dry paper to reveal the red plastic underneath to give the appearance of well-weathered brickwork where the face of the bricks has fallen off.

Lostwithiel's dairy has been made using adapted Walther's components.

At Golant a Class 22 B-B hydraulic leads a rake of empty clay wagons back down the branch to Lostwithiel. The background is taken from the real location.

Work-stained Collett '38XX' 3832 looks just the part with its train of china clay 'hoods'.

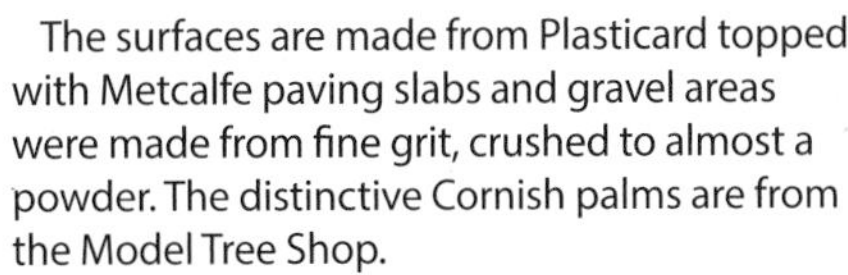

The surfaces are made from Plasticard topped with Metcalfe paving slabs and gravel areas were made from fine grit, crushed to almost a powder. The distinctive Cornish palms are from the Model Tree Shop.

Scenery is made from Modroc, painted dark brown and Woodland Scenics fine turf applied.

Adds Rob: "I have settled on a late summer theme and used the Burnt Grass colour as it's quite subdued and tones in nicely with the track work. In my opinion, there's nothing worse than overly bright or lurid grass on layouts."

Trees are a mix of homemade sea foam, commercially available brass etches and cheap examples bought online.

The River Fowey runs past the station at Lostwithiel and follows the branch line for the entire journey down to Fowey/Carne Point, and it was a natural feature of the layout, made using Woodland Scenics Deep Pour.

Lostwithiel has a distinctive 13th century bridge over the River Fowey, between the station and the main town. Although there wasn't space for the full five arch structure, Rob compromised on a two arch laser cut bridge made by Ancorton Models, which also includes cutwaters – triangular projections for pedestrian refuge.

> *"I was lucky enough that my wife agreed so long as she got a sewing room as well."*
>
> **ROB ELLIOTT**

American Imports

Buildings are mainly from the Bachmann Scenecraft (incuding wooden goods shed) and Hornby Lyddle End resin ranges.

Lostwithiel's distinctive platform mounted signal box is made from two Ratio kits joined together on a scratch-built brick base.

The original station buildings at Lostwithiel and Fowey were both wooden structures, but for now, Ratio stone built kits have been used until something more suitable can be procured.

Walthers Cornerstone range of modular buildings were used for the dairy building. "Despite it being American in its original design, I used the Red Wing Milling kit as a base and played about with it until it resembled a British looking concrete building," Rob explains. "After adding some P&D Marsh aluminium storage tanks, various bits of pipework, brass railings and a concrete base, it looks the part."

The Walthers range was also used for the china clay facilities along the dockside, based around the corrugated New River Mining kit, modified using brass etch and plastic girder to create three separate structures resembling the loading terminal. The structures are all roughly based on the originals at Carne Point. »

The unusual wagon tipplers represent those which were used to tip the clay out of wagons onto conveyor belts to be loaded onto ships. These were built from rail encased in Plasticard and brass strip mounted on small brass hinges. The traverser was built in a similar way.

All semaphore signals are Ratio kits, with a few parts from Model Signal Engineering and the latticework on the bracket signals is from Scalelink Fretcetera.

Rob also took the plunge by making his own point rodding, something not otfen modelled in 'OO' gauge, let alone 'N'.

Clay Days

"I was especially pleased when Farish produced its clay wagons for Kernow Model Rail Centre a few years ago – both the flat tarpaulin and clay hood variety," says Rob with no less enthusiasm than for his host of highly detailed locomotives and carriages of recent times. "A couple of rakes spend a lot of time trundling up the branch line to Carne Point and back. The plastic sheets are still a little bulky for my liking so I made my own using thin cigarette paper, donated by one of my local club members at Lichfield District Model Railway Society."

All rolling stock is either Farish or Dapol with the one exception being a Peco 'Collett Goods' 0-6-0.

As well as having fire irons, crew, brass lamp irons and real coal added, all stock is weathered, and all trains run with head lamps/discs and tail lamps.

Several people have contributed to Lostwithiel's success, not least Rob's wife Ruth, "for allowing a whole room in the house dedicated to trains", he remarks. "I appreciate how lucky I am in that regard." ■

READ MORE

Visit www.keymodelworld.com

Above: **A commendably clean Collett '68XX' 6837 *Forthampton Grange* heaves a mixed goods along the main line as china clay empties return from Fowey.**

Below: **The end of the Fowey branch scene includes the station and Carne Point clay docks. A pair of Dapol '57XX' 0-6-0PTs simmer in the yard after arriving with empty wagons while a '14XX' 0-4-2T pauses in the station behind with an autocoach.**

LOSTWITHIEL TRACK DIAGRAM (NOT TO SCALE)

9ft

5ft 6in

9ft

6ft

KEY			
1 Dairy	5 Station building	9 Golant	13 Unloading facilities
2 Level crossing	6 Goods yard	10 Carne Point clay docks	14 Tipplers
3 Houses	7 River Fowey	11 Fowey station	15 Traverser
4 Lostwithiel station	8 Fowey branch	12 Clay docks	

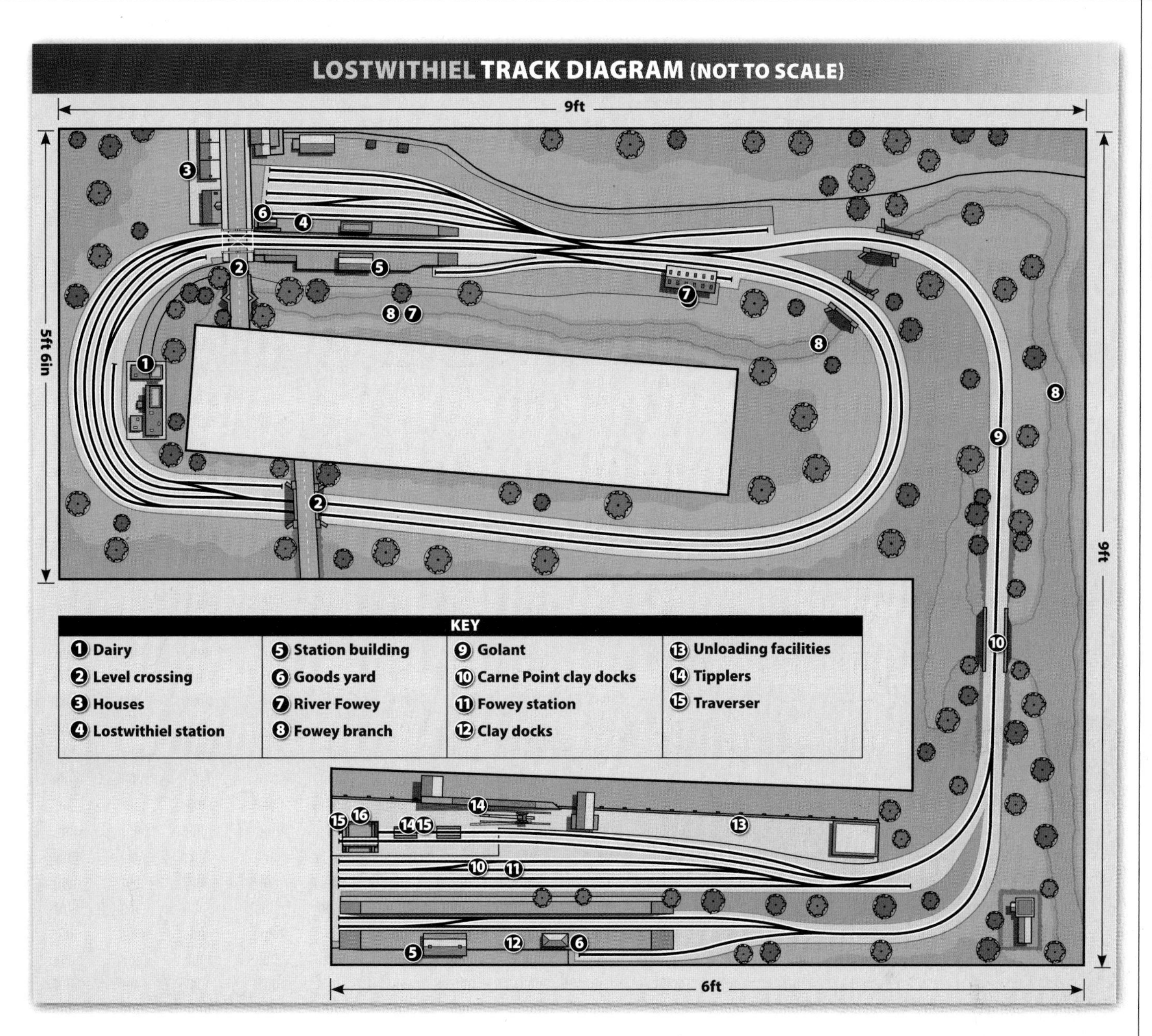

The double track main line scene provides a perfect place to watch trains pass snake through the landscape. A Graham Farish 'Warship' takes a parcels working around the continuous run section.

Tal-y-bont

After many years as a niche scale, 'OO9' is now very much accessible to all, thanks to some high fidelity ready-to-run products. **STEVE JONES** has taken full advantage to create a delightful narrow gauge railway set in Snowdonia.

Wharf station is modelled on Tywyn and uses a familar Peco station kit together with walling from Wills plastic sheets. The track has been embedded into the ground with Das modelling clay.

In the past, 'OO9' was the preserve of those willing and able to build locomotive kits and scratchbuilders. With new ready-to-run locomotives and rolling stock, the gauge will appeal to many more, particularly those challenged with limited space.

That's certainly the view of Steve Jones, someone who has built some beautiful layouts in 'OO', standard gauge but for whom Tal-y-bont was a first stab at narrow gauge.

"I've admired many layouts in the scale and it's difficult to beat a visit to a narrow gauge railway for charm and the scenery that they tend to run through – particularly those that run through the spectacular landscape of North Wales."

Bachmann's Baldwin 2-6-2T proved to be the catalyst to start his project.

"With a couple of points and some Peco flexible track, I began planning on the dining room table with a roll of lining paper and a pencil.

"The beauty of 'OO9'," he adds, "is that you can fit tons into a small space".

It was Steve's intention for the railway to run over a small viaduct similar to that at Dolgoch Falls on the Talyllyn Railway (TR). From that rough idea, a suitable name was researched which would be a nod to the world's first preserved railway, while making it clear that it wasn't a slavish model (especially as the TR is 2ft 3in gauge, whereas 'OO9' represents 1ft 11 1/2in).

War Department branded Baldwin 778 emerges from the tunnel and crosses the viaduct with a short demonstration goods train for Wharf station.

Tal-y-bont (meaning tall bridge in Welsh) "seemed appropriate and fitted the bill".

The idea is that the line is one now of the preserved, yet undiscovered, 'Great Little Trains of Wales', running through spectacular scenery, deep into the mountains of Snowdonia. »

Steve Jones' layout might be based on the style of the Talyllyn Railway, but its the long-dismantled Glyn Valley Tramway that comes to the fore as side-skirted Beyer, Peacock 0-4-2T Glyn traverses the scenic section between the two Tal-y-bont stations.

TAL-Y-BONT TRACK DIAGRAM (NOT TO SCALE)

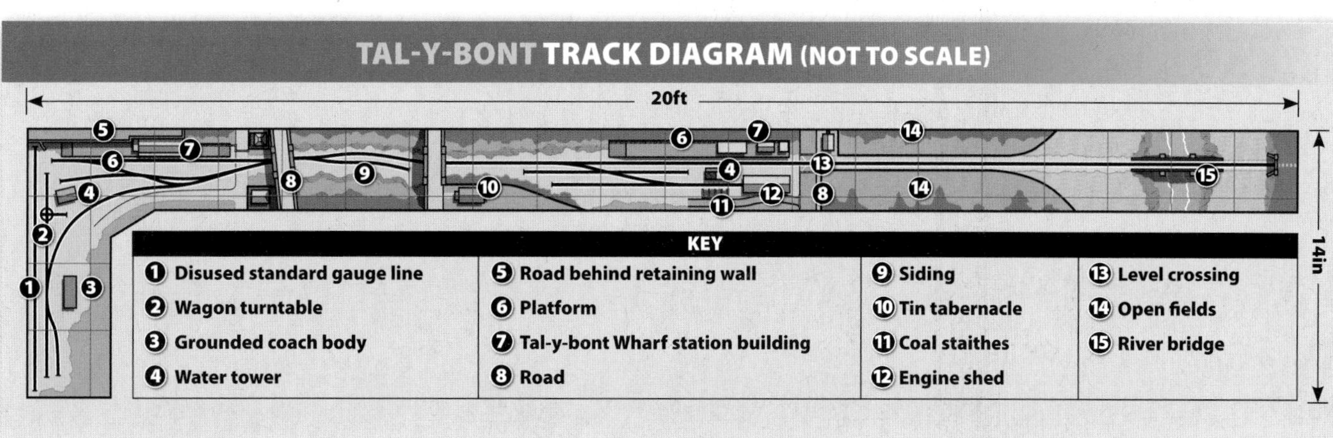

The line was built to transport slate to the main line at Tal-y-bont Wharf where it was transferred to standard gauge wagons for onward transportation to docks for shipment overseas, or to roof the houses of British towns and cities.

"I appreciate this is the story of almost every narrow-gauge line in North Wales," Steve continues, "but I like to build layouts that have credibility".

Station to station

The track plan for Tal-y-bont Wharf is copied from Tywyn on the TR, a terminus run-round facility and added interest of a standard gauge line (modelled as a disused piece of track) with derelict loading platform, wagon turntable, watering and coaling facility.

A Peco station building provides the narrow gauge station facilities, with a Wills water tower and crossing keeper's cottage for company. The bridge is scratch-built from Peco and Slaters plasticard. »

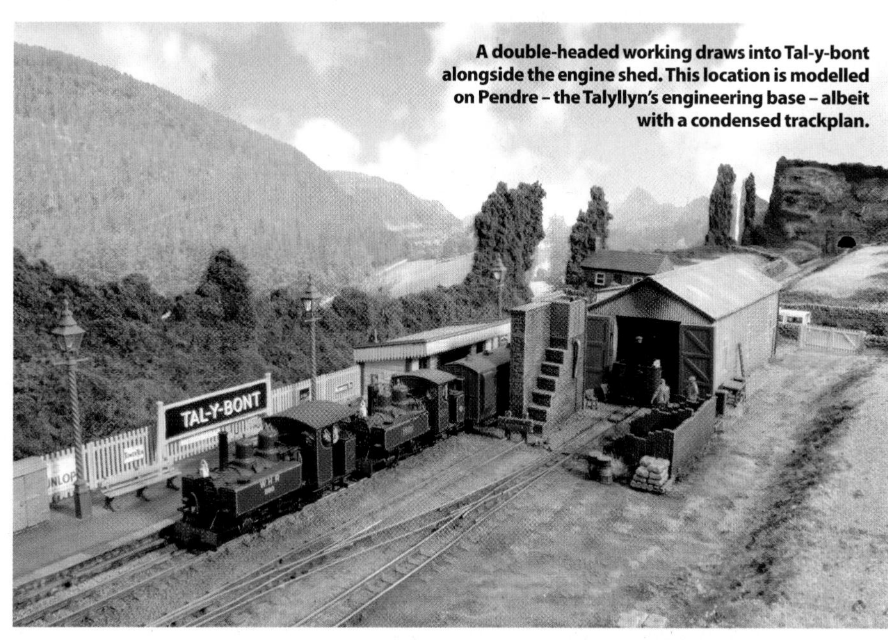

A double-headed working draws into Tal-y-bont alongside the engine shed. This location is modelled on Pendre – the Talyllyn's engineering base – albeit with a condensed trackplan.

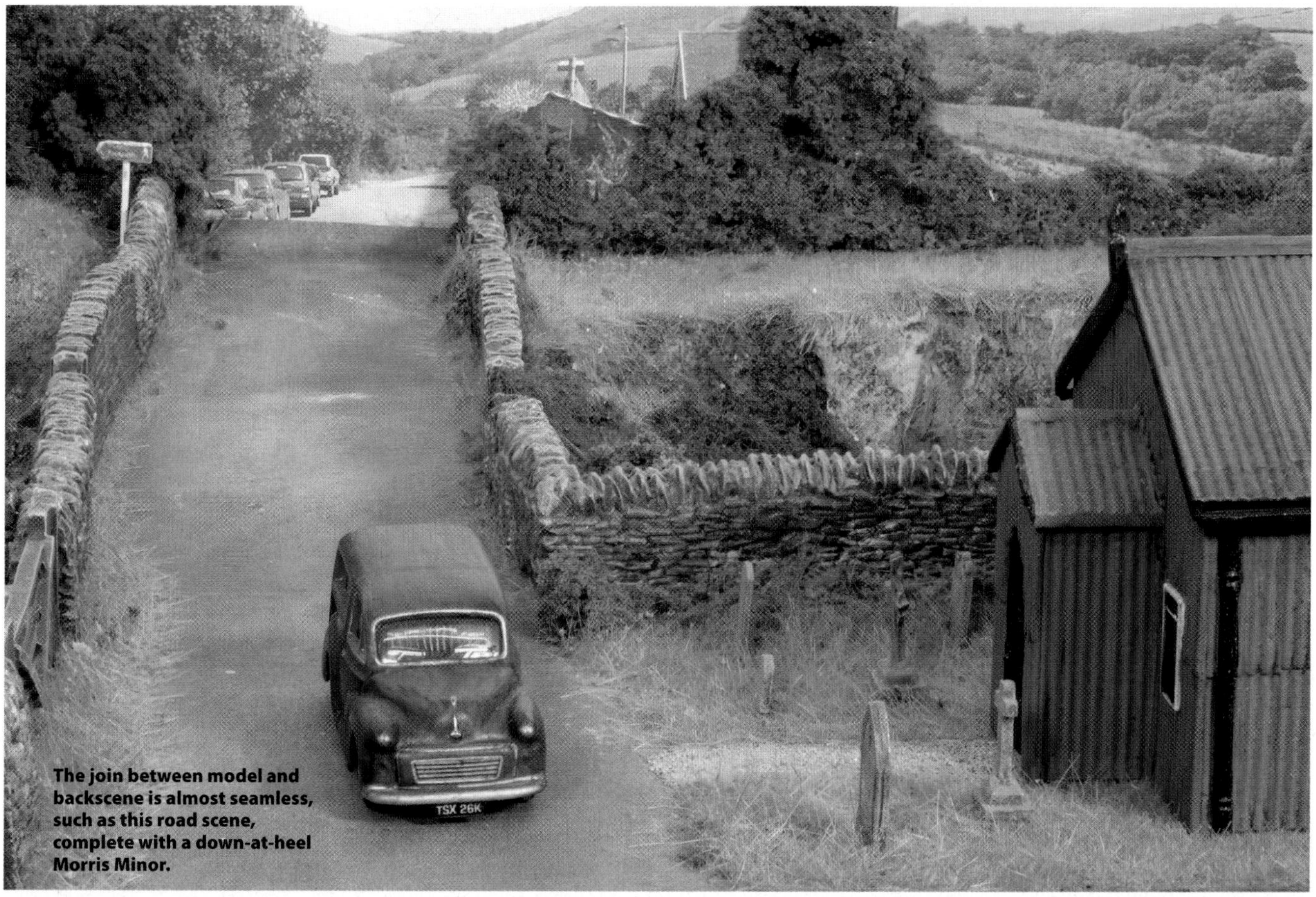

The join between model and backscene is almost seamless, such as this road scene, complete with a down-at-heel Morris Minor.

"I wanted to try to model a yard area and used DAS modelling clay to create the ground cover base layer, giving the impression of track embedded in all the associated dust, ash and muck," explains Steve. "You have to be brave and it can look a heck of a mess until it's dried and painted."

Tourist trains make their way through open countryside and a rock cutting for a modest distance to the next station. A small road bridge and the Wills 'tin tabernacle' church add scenic focus as we arrive at Tal-y-bont.

Inspiration came from Pendre, again on the Talyllyn, where its shed and maintenance facilities are located. The track plan on the model has been considerably trimmed down from the current form at Pendre, which in reality includes carriage sidings and extensive maintenance facilities.

"Even in 'OO9', compromise is still a necessity!" Steve cautions.

"As at Pendre, there is a level crossing and again, this is a feature I wanted to include. A motorised kit was sourced from Heathcote Electronics is powered by servos and a single

Hi-vis jackets confirm this is a preserved rather than historic railway scene.

Above: **Ex-Glyn Valley Tramway 0-4-2T eases into Wharf with a passenger service, adding variety to the otherwise Baldwin-dominated locomotive fleet.**

Left: **Tal-y-bont Viaduct - the emblematic image of the line. The background images were taken on a trip to Pistyll Rhaeadr Falls near Oswestry while the water effects are made with Woodland Scenics products.**

"The beauty of 'OO9' is that you can fit tons into a small space."

STEVE JONES

switch – very clever stuff if a little challenging to actually get working reliably."

Bachmann Scenecraft buildings (engine shed, water tower, ground frame box and cottage) add to the atmosphere, with another Peco station building providing the facilities for the passengers, predominantly Modelu products.

Departing eastwards, a Wills 'N' gauge stone viaduct carries the railway across a deep, open gorge, inspired by Dolgoch.

New gauge, fresh ideas

"I always like to try something new on a project and I liked the idea of modelling 'moving' water and a waterfall," says Steve. "I spent some time online watching experts creating some amazing water effects with Woodland Scenics products. The 'water' is a two-part resin mixture and relatively straightforward to use.

"There are various colours but I plumped for the murky water mix. My only advice though, is to make sure your riverbed is water tight: mine was not! It will find any way it can to leak out and I ended up with a puddle under the base-board on the dining room table!

"The Woodland Scenics 'water effects' was then used to create the waterfall and ripples on the surface once the resin had set."

The backscene is effectively a collage of scenes taken on Steve's phone while riding along up and down the Talyllyn Railway, having then been edited to obtain the optimum, matching sizes and compositions. Awkward transitions are disguised by bushes and trees.

To complete the visible part of its journey, trains finally plunge into an Peco 'N' gauge tunnel mouth, the exit to the 'rest of the world', or rather, the fiddle yard.

Steve concludes that he has "thoroughly enjoyed" the 'OO9' experience, but does warn anyone entering the narrow gauge world that "track, wheels and pick-ups must be spotless for reliable running". ■

READ MORE

Visit www.keymodelworld.com

DONCASTER

He grew up trainspotting at Doncaster station, then spent a career working at the town's famous 'Plant'. No guesses therefore for the location of **JOHN WHITE'S** ultimate dream layout!

"I can still vividly picture it now," John White reminisces. "A young lad wearing long trousers for the first time, with mouth open staring at the blue 'Deltic' humming away waiting for the all clear; I was in awe of this magnificent beast! I was well and truly hooked.

"It was the spring of 1959 and I was stood on a chilly Doncaster station where I was about to embark on a family visit to London. It was at that point I saw my first sighting of a DP1 Deltic on the front of our train."

Growing up within earshot of Doncaster Carr Loco and its adjacent marshalling yards and free time spent spotting on the station cemented the interest.

"On the occasions when my pocket money was low I had to settle for second best, standing in the adjacent cattle dock... I didn't mind though as I was still getting my fix!"

Express coming through... Thompson 'A2/2' 60505 *Thane of Fife* hurries south through Doncaster station's centre roads, watched by a Sulzer 'Class 24'.

Most of the locomotives on shed were built a stone's throw away at 'The Plant', with odd exceptions, like Stanier '8F' 48045, which was turned out from Vulcan Foundry in Newton-le-Willows, Lancashire.

Indeed, John already had railway blood running through his veins. His father and uncles had all worked at the town's famous works, known as 'The Plant'.

And so it was that John secured an apprenticeship at Doncaster in 1966 as an electrician, including work at the Crimsall Workshops with 'Deltics', '37s' and '31s', finishing his time re-wiring the 'Class 83' electrics.

On a roll

A lifelong fascination with model railways resulted in the perhaps inevtable conlcusion that John would seek to relive his past through a model of 'Donny', withe changeover steam to diesel period of 1959-1966.

"Most people when looking for a new property tend to concentrate on which way the garden faces, but my focus was looking for the roof space for a conversion into a large room for future railway projects," he says.

This enabled a generous 37ft x 12ft space to do justice to the sprawling East Coast Main Line (ECML) hub in 'OO'.

Construction of the baseboards used a 3in x 1in soft wood for the frame and 11mm plywood on the top, with all joints screwed and glued. The main station boards are 3ft deep and the fiddle yards 2ft. »

"I can really lose myself when in the railway room, sat at the control of a named express."

JOHN WHITE

Left: **Gresley V2 60828 has skirted around Doncaster station with a lengthy train of Conflats, rejoining the main line from the avoiding lines. Note the working oil lamps.**

Below: **Main line modelling on a grand scale. All manner of trains converge in an especially busy moment at Doncaster.**

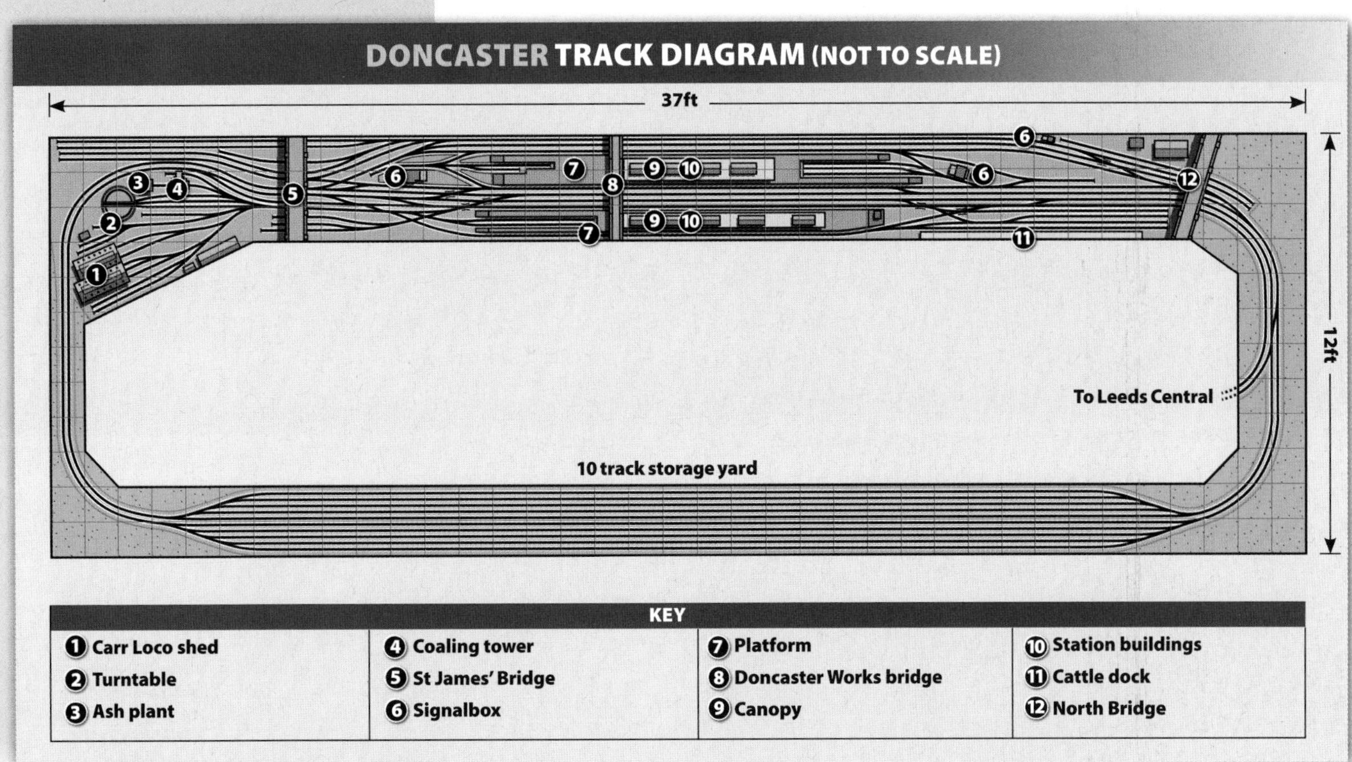

All have at least three cross supports for added strength and preventing twisting.

Before laying any track, the ply was covered with 2mm thick rubber-foam underlay, following successful experimentation with leftovers from a wooden flooring project.

The trackplan was traced onto a large roll paper, although the overall station width needed reducing to fit the space available, resulting in the removal of one track between Platforms 7/8 and reducing the number of avoiding lines from five to two.

DCC control was standarised from the outset, with a small percentage of locomotives fitted with sound. Track is Peco's reliable Code 75 with electrofrog points.

Scene setting

Structures are mainly scratch built with the odd exception.

The main station buildings were made with artist's plastic form board, made in box sections and covered with brick paper, inserted with doors and windows. Its roof line is topped-off with Ratio roof tiles together with Metcalfe grey roofing. Canopies on the station are by Hornby with improved glazing.

Doncaster's steam-era signal boxes were situated at each end of the station (North and South Box) and are represented using Bachmann Scenecraft items, even if they are not exactly the correct design and may be replaced in time.

The station environs are flanked by scratch-built modes of St James' and North bridges. Meanwhile, access to 'The Plant' is via the instantly recognisable girder bridge, which John used to cross every morning at 07:15 on his way to the Crimpsall. Some may recognise its 'OO' re-creation which started out as the famous Airfix kit. »

A schoolboy 'spotter' improvises to make sure he doesn't miss out on any of the action.

Left: **Crewe built (later, ironically Doncaster scrapped) 'Class 24/1' D5082 stands beneath the girder bridge walkway that saw millions of workers arrive and depart the town's major railway works.**

Below: **A locomotive paradise! Even in compresses form, John White' Doncaster Carr depot is still impressive.**

Peppercorn 'A1' and 'K1' designs arrive simultaneously with their respective express and semi-fast services from the north.

Automatic colour light signals that sequence from green to red sequencing back to single amber/double, amber/green and green is triggered sensors under the track.

In order to accommodate Carr Loco, the steam depot, one mile south of the station required some significant space compression compromise, achieved by missing out the trackwork between St James' Bridge and Balby Bridge. Indeed, the depot itself covered many acres of land so this had to be reduced and re-configured to fit.

The main running shed was purchased from a toy fair as, by luck, it looked very similar to the prototype. The turntable is Heljan, coaling tower is Bachmann and the ash plant scratch-built.

Well stocked

The majority of the locomotive fleet is provided Bachmann, Hornby and Heljan with several modified steam locomotives to add variety.

A particular highlight is 'A1/1' 60113 *Great Northern*, a much altered Hornby 'A3', which was completed by John's friend Graeme King. The chassis had the front bogie repositioned, new resin cylinders, custom-etched valve gear, resin smokebox and deflectors, and adapted cabsides.

All locomotives are suitably fitted with lamps with authentic headcodes.

Carriage rakes are mainly fixed, all fitted with short tension lock couplings to close unsightly gaps between the coaches. Each set is fitted with Kaydee couplings at both ends; track magnets are placed between the tracks (some disguised as a barrow crossing) at strategic locations for uncoupling.

Time afforded by retirement has provided John the opportunity to enjoy his favourite pastime: "operating my railway".

"I can really lose myself when in the railway room, sat at the control of a named express being pulled by a 'Streak'," he continues. "What a sheer delight!"

Doncaster is operated in progressive time zones from 1959 to 1966.

"I start a session by operating a full steam only timetable, then slowly introducing the diesel element, until the transition is complete. This can take up to several days depending on family commitments."

Leeds united

One of John's former exhibition layouts, Leeds Central, is positioned in the centre of Doncaster layout., meaning that a service can be operated between the two Yorkshire conurbations.

Many services from Leeds/York/Hull stopped at Doncaster where they would then be shunted together to travel to London as one formation, something the layout's maker strives to replicate by bringing a four coach Pullman set behind a 'B1' or 'V1/3' into Platform 1. Another six-coach Pullman then rolls in behind a 'Pacific' (usually an 'A1') into Platform 4. The 'B1'/'V1/3' uncouples and goes on shed as the 'A1' reforms the two dining trains as one.

The station also witnesses many other exchanges, including passenger and goods, which ensures the entire motive power fleet is used.

As if two running two connected ECML railway centres in one room wasn't enough, John has plans to build a fictitious diesel depot for that "ever-growing" fleet! ■

READ MORE

Visit www.keymodelworld.com

Twelve Trees Junction

Bulleid generations meet as 1-Co-Co-1 10201 powers towards the station as 'Merchant Navy' 35017 *Belgian Marine* heads for the south west with a heavy Pullman train. The Brighton Belle EMU adds a further touch of opulence.

The *Hornby Magazine* team has never been afraid of taking on a big project. Twelve Trees remains one of its most popular, even after a decade on the exhibition circuit. **MIKE WILD** outlines the trains…

Drummond 'M7' 0-4-4T 30029 rolls to a stop in the bay platform with a Maunsell push-pull set for passenger to change over the multiple unit on the main line.

Twelve Trees Junction is one of *Hornby Magazine*'s biggest exhibition layouts and also its longest serving.

At 24ft x 10ft, it is a substantial model and it needs a large collection of locomotives and rolling stock to make it function properly during an exhibition weekend.

Construction started in late 2011, but it wasn't until 2013 that things really got underway with a brand new trackplan. Even then the layout was only a set of four 4ft x 3ft scenic baseboards without storage yards and it was another year before the full scheme was completed to allow it to make its debut at the Great Electric Train Show in October 2014.

In that format, the full size was 34ft x 8ft, and to make it work, three cassette storage yards were made to facilitate the operation of the main through lines and diverging route.

Twelve Trees stayed in its 34ft format until 2017 when the team decided it was time that we rebuilt the layout into a continuous run to make it more enjoyable to operate.

The original cassette yard boards were therefore repurposed, as well as building new corner boards for the storage yard and creating potential for future expansion with two new scenic sections at the front.

The biggest impact with the design change was that more rolling stock could be showcased and operation of the the layout was more fluent. With the old system there could be pauses in the service while trains were over, but with the new continuous run storage yard a more consistent pace of trains could be delivered as they passed through the scenic section as well as making the most of the complex junction trackplan.

Stock take

Twelve Trees has featured in the magazine and yearbooks several times, so it's time to take a fresh angle, this time the eclectic range of stock that occupies its vast fiddle yard.

Over the past two decades, interest in the Southern Region has reached an all-time high, assisted by the huge range of motive power »

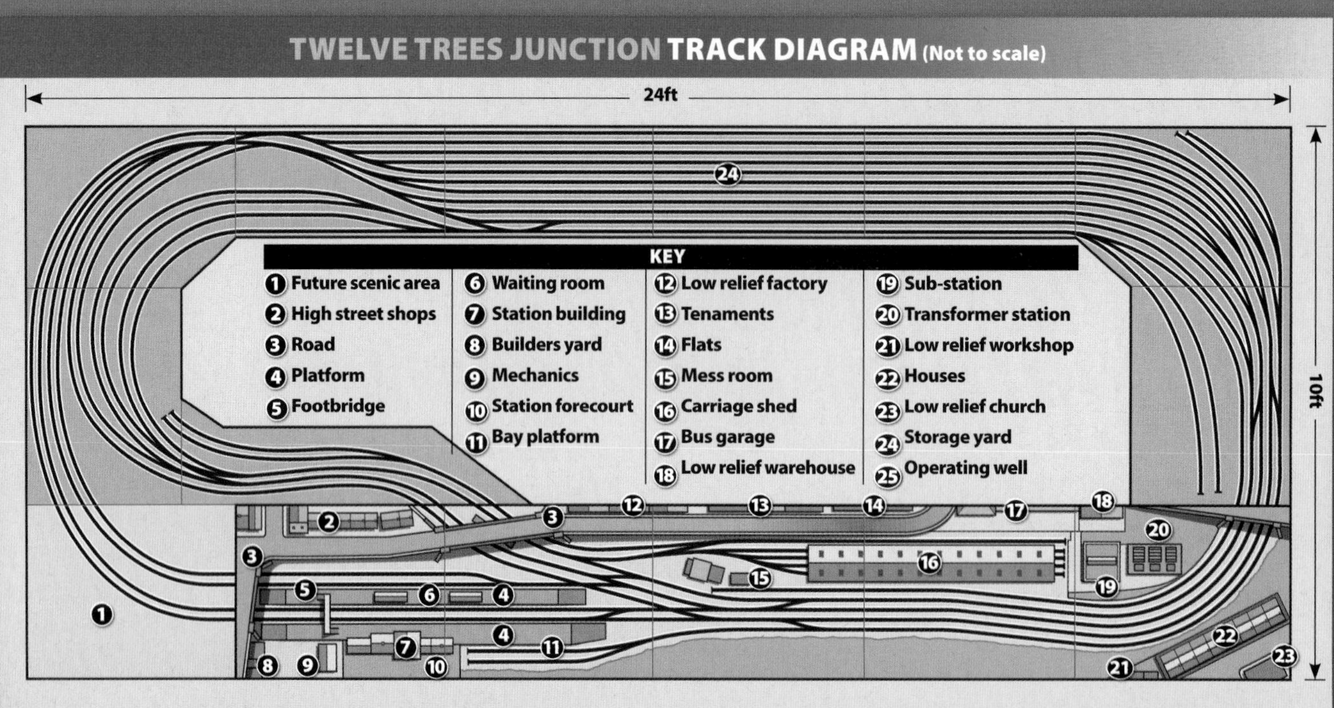

now available off-the-shelf. No other region offers the same spread of steam, diesel and electric traction running side by side, which is one of the great appeals of the Southern – and indeed, hopefully, the layout.

Hornby has been prolific in creating outstanding ready-to-run Southern Railway/Region locomotives with recent highlights including its air-smoothed Bulleid 'Merchant Navy' 4-6-2s, Maunsell 'Lord Nelson' 4-6-0, Maunsell 'S15' 4-6-0 and even the humble Adams '0415' 4-4-2T.

Steam is at the heart of the fleet for Twelve Trees and reflects the final decade of its service between 1957 and 1967. Covering this period allows the collection to be quite diverse, as we can include Drummond, Urie, Adams and Maunsell designs alongside the latest generation of steam locomotives from Bulleid and Riddles.

All of the steam locomotives which form part of the exhibition roster are sound fitted

Immaculate 'Lord Nelson' 30863 *Lord Rodney* coasts under the main road, crossing paths with a similarly well kept '2-HAL' EMU.

Bulleid rebuilt 'Merchant Navy' 4-6-2 35017 *Belgian Marine* passes straight through the station with a Pullman working in between a variety of multiple units. From the left are a 2-H DEMU, together with 2-EPB, 4-SUB and 4-EPB EMUs.

using a combination of ZIMO, ESU and now Doehler & Haass chips to bring them to life. Each of these uses a suitable speaker while three of the air-smoothed 'West Country' 4-6-2s and the 'Golden Arrow' decorated 'Britannia' 4-6-2 are also equipped with smoke generators.

Among the latest additions to the fleet are Hornby's air-smoothed 'Merchant Navy' 4-6-2s modelling 35023 *Holland Afrika Line* and 35028 *Clan Line* in BR lined green. Both are fitted with ZIMO sound decoders while 35028 features firebox glow and working electric cab lights.

There is also a Hornby 'S15' on the roster finished as 30843 and suitably weathered to make it the perfect addition to the head of long goods trains.

A Drummond '700' 0-6-0 has been detailed with a coal load, crew, ZIMO sound decoder and weathering. This is perfect engine for the ballast train or the newly added Bachmann steam crane in Southern Region black.

Bulleid 'Q1' 0-6-0 33023 has Locoman Sounds' new Southern Region two-cylinder sound file for the Doehler & Haass 8-pin decoder.

The late steam era collection features more BR Standards with the '3MT' and '4MT' tanks being joined by a pair of '4MT' 2-6-0s, occasionally a '4MT' 4-6-0 and '5MT' 4-6-0 73082 *Camelot*. There are also two rebuilt 'Merchant Navy' 4-6-2s – 35017 *Belgian Marine* with a Locoman Sounds decoder and 35025 *Brocklebank Line* with a South West Digital ESU chip.

The steam roster isn't limited to big engines. A range of tank engines is available, including a trio of 0-4-4Ts which are used on the push-pull trains from the bay platform. These are Drummond 'M7' 0-4-4T 30029 fitted with an ESU decoder and a Howes sound file together; Wainwright 'H' 0-4-4T 31518 and Adams 'O2' 0-4-4T 30182, all of which have ZIMO MX648 decoders and Digitrains sound files. Technically it would have been rare to see the 'H' from the South Eastern section alongside the 'M7' and 'O2', but the joy of modelling means reality can be skewed a little.

A Bachmann Billinton 'E4' 0-6-2T – again fitted with a ZIMO sound chip – works alongside the likes of a BR '3MT' 2-6-2T and '4MT' 2-6-4T on lighter passenger formations, as well as empty stock movements.

Electric overload

A key feature of Twelve Trees' roster is the large collection of electric locomotives and multiple units that have been amassed over the years. One of the most popular additions has been the Class 71 electrics which we, between us, now have six available for the layout with a combination of the currently available Hornby model and the now out-of-production DJ Models product in service.

These include E5015 with full 'Golden Arrow' regalia, a heavily weathered E5022 which is usually at the head of a block train of Ferry »

Bachmann's superb LBSCR modular station building set, based on Sheffield Park, also makes for an ideal main line scene.

Vans and E5001 in BR green with small yellow warning panels.

The Class 71s are joined by an expanding fleet of Dapol Class 73s. Since their release, three have been added to the roster – E6001 in BR green with small yellow warning panels, E6003 in BR green with a grey solebar plus E6022 in BR blue with small yellow warning panels.

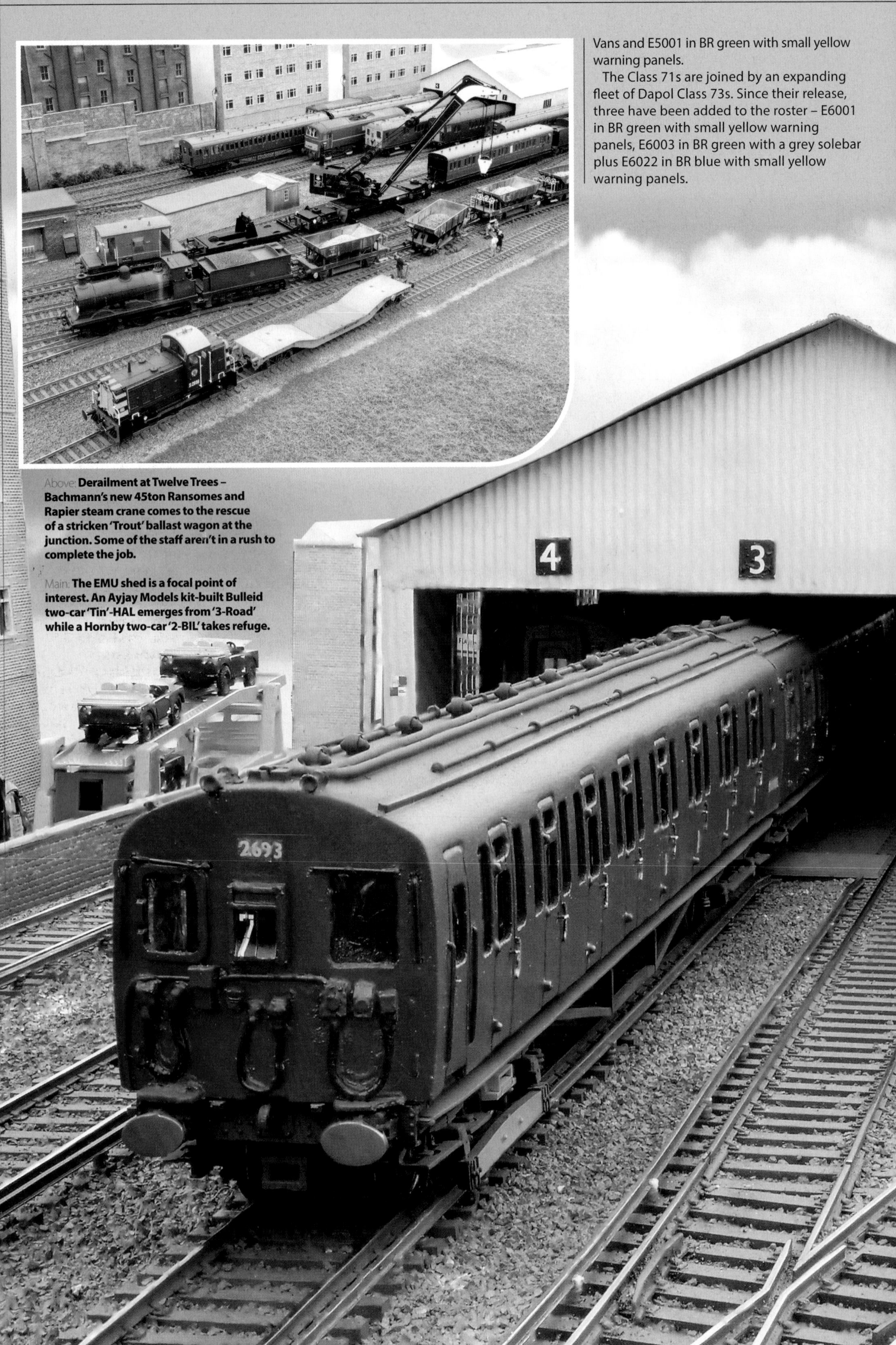

Above: **Derailment at Twelve Trees – Bachmann's new 45ton Ransomes and Rapier steam crane comes to the rescue of a stricken 'Trout' ballast wagon at the junction. Some of the staff aren't in a rush to complete the job.**

Main: **The EMU shed is a focal point of interest. An Ayjay Models kit-built Bulleid two-car 'Tin'-HAL emerges from '3-Road' while a Hornby two-car '2-BIL' takes refuge.**

Alongside the electrics there are a handful of diesels including a pair of Class 33/0s with ZIMO decoders, which are normally coupled at the head of Heljan Class B tankers, complete with barrier wagons, or a block train of Presflo cement wagons. Accurascale's Cemflo wagons will also join the fleet for exhibitions, but they are currently awaiting weathering.

A third 'Crompton', Class 33/1 D6580 in BR green, is modified with push-pull equipment to run with 4-TC units. It always operates in tandem with a Kernow Model Rail Centre 4-TC unit and the pairing has Legomanbiffo sound decoders installed which work together.

However, the most significant part of the electric fleet are the multiple units. No model of the Southern Region third-rail network would be complete without them and it is quite staggering to realise how much is now available off the shelf.

The fleet consists of four Bachmann 4-CEPs, four Bachmann 2-EPBs, multiples of the Hornby 2-BIL and 2-HAL units, plus three 4-VEPs, a 4-TC and two 'Brighton Belle' units in ready-to-run form.

There are modified and kit built units too including a BR 4-EPB - built by reworking a pair of Bachmann 2-EPBs – and an Ayjay Models 4-SUB unit which have been renovated and equipped with decoders, extra pick-ups and stay alive capacitors for improved running.

Not quite electric, but still in the same category, are a trio of Class 205 2-H Diesel Electric Multiple Units (DEMUs) in plain green, green with an orange triangle on the guard's end cab front and green with small yellow warning panels.

"Twelve Trees Junction still has an extensive job list for the future, both for its rolling stock and the layout."

Passenger stock

When Twelve Trees was first built, the range of passenger stock available was restricted to four main types: Bachmann's Mk 1s and Bulleid 63ft main line corridor stock together with Hornby's eight-wheel Pullmans and its collection of Maunsell 59ft stock.

Since then, the line-up has been expanded to include a full rake of Hornby 12-wheel Pullmans to model the 'Bournemouth Belle'.

There has also been the addition of Bachmann 'Birdcage' carriages, Hornby's rebuilt LSWR 58ft non-corridor carriages, the Maunsell Second Open and Restaurant car, LSWR 'Gate stock' push-pull carriages from Kernow Model Rail Centre/EFE and Hornby's Bulleid 59ft 'Shortie' suburban corridor stock.

Twelve Trees Junction still has an extensive job list for the future both for its rolling stock and the layout. There are still locomotives, units, carriages and wagons to enter service following weathering and sound installation while undoubtedly there will be new additions to make our Southern scene even more realistic.

Happily, the layout will remain long-lasting part of the *Hornby Magazine* layout collection for the foreseeable future. ■

READ MORE

Visit www.keymodelworld.com

A Maunsell 'Schools' 4-4-0 leads a Bachmann 'Birdcage' set and passes a 'T9' 4-4-0 with a trio of Hornby 58ft Maunsell non-corridor coaches.